RANDOM
ACTS OF
KINDNESS

ALSO BY DETE MESERVE

Good Sam
Perfectly Good Crime
The Space Between

PRAISE FOR
GOOD SAM

"Meserve's narrative has a... dry wit and well-conceived dialogue throughout. Kate's relatable qualities of self-reliance tinged with vulnerability drive this gratifying mystery-romance about finding the good guys—and knowing when to recognize them."

—Publishers Weekly

"In her debut novel, Meserve writes a... solid feel-good romance sparked with mystery."

—Kirkus Reviews

"If you are a Nicholas Sparks or Richard Paul Evans fan, I'm betting you will like author Meserve's book *Good Sam*. Uplifting, heart wrenching, and a two-hankie read, this story is a winner."

—Cheryl Stout, Amazon top reviewer and Vine Voice

"This story had everything from suspense to drama. And the heartfelt ending had us smiling for days."

—First for Women magazine

PRAISE FOR
PERFECTLY GOOD CRIME

"A first-rate and undaunted protagonist easily carries this brisk tale. Kate is intuitive and professional, but it's her steadfast compassion that makes her truly remarkable."

—*Kirkus Reviews*

"Dete Meserve delivers a novel that is simultaneously mysterious, fascinating, and inspiring."

—BuzzFeed.com

"A feel-good mystery… an enjoyable escape."

—BookLife Prize in Fiction

"Books that are changing the world."

—2016 Living Now Book Award,
gold medal in inspirational fiction

"In a story saturated with unexpected twists and shocking motives, Kate Bradley follows clues—and her heart—to discover that some crimes have powerfully good intentions."

—*Sunset* magazine

PRAISE FOR
THE SPACE BETWEEN

"Chiseled prose gleefully weaves the protagonist through bombshells… A labyrinth of plot and character motivations makes for a thoroughly enjoyable novel."

—*Kirkus Reviews*

"*The Space Between* is a fast-paced novel that combines the best elements of suspense and romance. In this story of a broken marriage, Dete Meserve uses the mysteries of the universe to keep you on the edge of your seat as she weaves a tale that winds its way through the past and present to bring about a truly satisfying conclusion. Highly recommended."

—*USA Today* bestselling author
Bette Lee Crosby

"Woven with the stars, this is an incredible story of love, betrayal, and the infinite power of hope. Suspenseful to almost the last page; I couldn't put it down."

—Andrea Hurst,
author of *Always with You*

"From tragedy to triumph, Dete Meserve's new novel took me on a roller-coaster ride I'll not soon forget. Coupling the mysteries of the night sky with an unthinkable domestic situation, this tale is stunning and unlike any I've read. *The Space Between* is a must must must read!"

—Heather Burch,
bestselling author of *In the Light of the Garden*

"As captivating and complex as the night skies that feature in *The Space Between*, this is a thrilling read. A precipitous shift in perceived reality causes everything past and present to be suspect. Meserve skillfully crafts all the elements of a superbly suspenseful page-turner."

—Patricia Sands,
bestselling author of the Love in Provence series

"Dete Meserve's *The Space Between* has it all. It is a story written with a knowledge of space, realistic characters you want to root for, romance, and a mystery with a satisfying ending. I predict that after you read the book, you'll gaze at the stars and think of them in a new way."

—Judith Keim, bestselling author
of the Fat Fridays Group series

RANDOM ACTS OF KINDNESS

Inspiring True Stories

Dete Meserve
and Rachel Greco

MELROSE HILL PUBLISHING
Los Angeles, California

Published by Melrose Hill Publishing

www.DeteMeserve.com

ISBN- 978-0-9914499-7-2 (paperback)

ISBN- 978-0-0014499-6-5 (e-book)

Printed in the United States of America

This book is dedicated to
Good Samaritans everywhere,
who, through actions big and small,
bring light and hope into the world.

"No act of kindness, no matter how small, is ever wasted."

—Aesop

Contents

Foreword

RACHEL GRECO

I LOVE READING good news.

I love writing it too, but as a journalist working at the *Lansing State Journal*, covering several communities, I have to be comfortable being a jill-of-all-trades. I don't have the luxury of being choosy; I cover anything and everything: car crashes, fires, contentious school board and government decisions, deaths, dangerous weather conditions, and the occasional court case.

Still, every once in a while, I stumble upon someone helping a person in need, an extraordinary community effort, a heroic act, or a touching relationship that inspires people. I consider myself lucky because I've written numerous pieces about all those. In truth, they often get me through the sad and terrible things I've covered as a reporter.

I always look forward to telling these stories, just as many readers look forward to seeing them. They inspire, lift people up, lighten the soul. Some of them restore our faith in humanity.

A few years ago, I met a single mom and her two teenagers, and their story did all these things for me. The family lived in Potterville, a small community outside Lansing, Michigan.

I met with them because one of the teens had written an essay about his mother and entered it in a national contest in hopes of winning the family a new wheelchair-accessible van. His mother needed one, he told me. The stroke she had suffered several years earlier had limited her mobility. The van she drove was fifteen years old and in bad shape.

I sat in their living room and listened to their story. Although the teens discussed their family's need for a new van, they talked even more about their mom, who spent much of her time shuttling them to sports practices, games, and after-school activities. When the van broke down, which it often did, she always managed to scrape together enough money to keep it going, insistent that her children get where they needed to be.

She didn't just need a new van, they told me. She *deserved* one, because there'd never been a time when she hadn't put her children first.

We walked out to the driveway in front of their small manufactured house, all four of us, to take a look at their aging vehicle. The wheelchair lift at the back of the van was leaking hydraulic fluid and falling apart, and rust had eaten holes through the interior floor. In the winter, cold Michigan air rushed into the van, and from inside the vehicle, I saw the asphalt of the driveway below where the metal was missing.

I left the interview and drove back to work thinking about how gracious they were and how badly I wished I could help them secure that van.

The contest came and went. They didn't win.

That's when I received a phone call. The man on the line inquired about the single mother in need of a new van.

"Did she get it?" he asked.

I told him she hadn't.

"Then I'd like to buy her one," he said. "Could you help me find out what kind of wheelchair lift she needs?"

I agreed to call the woman and ask some basic questions about her wheelchair lift, but under the guise that another reporter at the paper was writing about wheelchair-accessible vehicles and needed the information. I didn't want to get her hopes up if the man couldn't live up to his promise.

But he did. Three months later the new van, worth $45,000, was ready.

Calling the family I'd interviewed to break the news about the gift is a moment I'll never forget. There were tears. Only some of them were mine.

A week later, I was in their driveway again, watching the Good Samaritan businessman and the single mother meet for the first time. Parked in the driveway was the new van. The man told me his gesture was important, not just for the mother he'd helped but also for him.

The experience brought two strangers together, and then it connected me with Dete Meserve, an author who feels just as strongly as I do about telling these kinds of heartwarming stories.

It also served as proof of all the good everyone is capable of.

Working with Dete, a writer who's chosen to tell stories of kindness, has been a joy.

The Good Sams I've met—and the impact they've made—are inspirational.

Most important, every one of them is a reminder that people are inherently good—that no matter the amount of ugliness, violence, and tragedy in the world, there are equal amounts of kindness and good, and much of it is the work of your neighbors, friends, coworkers, and people you've never met.

Small acts of goodwill are everywhere. They're powerful enough to change the world for the better. We can't forget them. We should, in fact, seek them out and hold on to them.

You'll read some of them here.

I hope you enjoy them and, by all means, let them lighten your soul.

Introduction

DETE MESERVE

MY PHONE CHIMES, alerting me to another email in my inbox. It dings with a Twitter notification. A Facebook message.

It will do this all day. Every day.

Gentle chimes that signal an act of kindness. And another story.

Well into the night, the messages arrive from people everywhere, all sharing stories about those who bring happiness and kindness to others. They always come with a joyful note:

"Can you believe what this little boy is doing?!"

"What a remarkable Good Sam this is!"

"Have your tissues handy, Dete!"

That's why I brought this book to life. I had to share the beautiful truth that despite what we see on the news, thousands of people are performing meaningful acts of kindness around the globe. Every day.

But the book's journey truly began when a friend shared an article, written by award-winning journalist Rachel Greco, about a Good Samaritan in Michigan who gave a disabled woman—a woman he'd never met—a new van. As I read the story, I got a lump in my throat, and tears stung the corners of my eyes: sure signs that the tale was awakening in me a powerful reminder of human kindness and compassion.

I reached out to Rachel and discovered a kindred spirit—and someone with whom to partner on this book. Rachel regularly covered troubling news about car crashes, house fires, and brutality, and she longed to write more stories about people who bring light and hope to others. Each week, as we culled through dozens of story ideas to consider for *Random Acts of Kindness*, we found ourselves in awe of the myriad of beautiful, surprising ways people help others.

These stories restore hope.

Certain kinds of heroes—firefighters, doctors, and paramedics—rush in when things go wrong. But the stories in *Random Acts of Kindness* spotlight ordinary people from age nine to one hundred who have found creative, inspiring, unique ways to give back and make a difference. Some of the stories will warm your heart and make you laugh; others will make you smile; and a few will make you cry—in a good way—with the joy of knowing there's so much goodness and kindness in the world.

Each of these stories is true and original. Rachel and I spent countless hours tracking down Good Sams, interviewing them, and writing stories to honor the spirit of what they were doing. Working on this book has made us profoundly aware of the boundless goodness all around us.

That's what we hope happens to you as you read this book. These stories are uplifting, joyous, and comforting. They'll restore your spirit and bring a smile to your face, whether you're going through a difficult time or practicing gratitude for all that's good and wondrous in your life.

We hope these stories also inspire you to be your best self and find gentle, loving, thoughtful ways to bring joy and hope to those you care about—or even complete strangers. "Each and every one of us can become a bright candle," Pope Francis once said, "a reminder that light will overcome darkness and never the other way around."

None of the Good Sams profiled in this book are famous—although they should be!—nor do they possess large sums of money or any special abilities. They're ordinary people who became extraordinary through making the world a better place—one random act of kindness at a time.

KINDNESS AT ANY AGE

Fraternity Boys Surprise Twelve-Year-Old Cancer Fighter

A SIGN GOES up in the corner of a hospital window, facing a frat house across the street.

CANCER FIGHTER, 12 YEARS OLD, WOULD LIKE A PIZZA. THANK YOU.

The next day, five fraternity brothers walk across the street with a pizza box. They ask for the girl's room number, ride the elevator, and greet her. They surround her hospital bed, hand her a dozen roses, and serenade her while one of them plays guitar.

That's how Lexi Brown's friendship with the brothers at Sigma Alpha Epsilon at the University of California, Los Angeles, began.

Local and national media covered the simple gesture.

It also made the rounds on social media—good news people couldn't get enough of.

The story was everywhere.

But why this act of kindness truly matters to Lexi, who's been battling an unforgiving cancer since age ten, and what it means to the UCLA students who know her, is much bigger.

And far from over.

A Small but Powerful Act

On a weekday afternoon in February, Lexi was making the three-hour drive from her family's home in Santa Maria to Mattel Children's Hospital at UCLA. On the trip, she joked with her mom, Lisa. They laugh with each other a lot; it's part of who Lexi is: funny, bright, athletic, competitive.

She was scheduled to undergo another round of chemotherapy there. There'd been so much chemotherapy in the last two years that Lisa had lost track of how many rounds Lexi had gone through. A bump, barely visible, on Lexi's left thigh, had given way to her initial cancer diagnosis.

Before the fraternity brothers visited with her at the hospital the previous fall, Lexi was at a low point in her battle. An oral medication she'd been taking had landed her in the emergency room. Lisa said her daughter's symptoms were frightening. Lexi, usually active and upbeat, was tired, cold, and struggling to sleep. At night her heart seemed to be "beating out of her chest," said Lisa.

In the ER, her heart rate spiked; she was suffering from acute heart failure. As a result, Lexi was airlifted to Mattel Children's Hospital.

The sign Lisa placed in the window was a whim, a distraction, something to do while they waited for Lexi to be well enough to go home.

"Let's make a sign asking for pizza," Lisa urged her daughter, who lay in her hospital bed. "Wouldn't it be cool if the fraternity brothers who live across the street saw this?"

Twenty-one-year-old Kevin Autran took note of it. Then acting president at Sigma Alpha Epsilon, he read the sign in the fifth-floor window and went to his fraternity brothers.

"You look out and see that sign in the window," he said. "I made all the other guys aware of it."

Lisa said her daughter got eleven pizza deliveries that day. Some were from friends, because Lexi's father, Jon, had posted a photo of the sign on social media. But others were from the UCLA campus police, other students, and strangers.

Then Sigma Alpha Epsilon arrived.

"At first I didn't really know what to think, except that I was really grateful," Lexi said.

Lisa stood back and watched in amazement. "I just started bawling my heart out," she said. "There were five guys there singing to my daughter. It was pretty powerful."

Kevin said when the group returned to the fraternity house after their visit with Lexi, they were changed. "It was so easy, but people don't appreciate what they can do with such a small act of kindness," he said. "It just felt good."

In the days that followed, the fraternity brothers paid frequent visits to Lexi's hospital room, playing games and chatting with her. Then they paid tribute to their newfound friendship with Lexi. The fraternity brothers decorated the roof of their house with lights that spelled out "LEXI." They finished the display with a flashing red heart. During her hospital stay the fraternity brothers brought her their fraternity flag and decorated her room. They introduced Lexi to dozens of university athletes, many who visited her room.

Kevin said Lexi is adorable but, more important, a fighter. "It's a hard situation, but the fact that she keeps her head up and stays positive says a lot about her."

The visits were so frequent that the hospital staff lifted visitor restrictions for the rest of Lexi's stay.

By the time she checked out of the hospital, Lexi had become friends with several UCLA students.

Close Friends, a Meaningful Connection

Today, Lexi undergoes chemotherapy at least once a week.

It's been months since she met the brothers at Sigma Alpha Epsilon, but many of their numbers are programmed into Lisa's phone. They call; they text; they visit the family.

"I consider them really close friends," Lexi said.

It isn't uncommon for a fraternity or sorority member to stop by her hospital room or the Browns' home for a game of cards. They bring makeup and nail polish. They invite Lexi to UCLA soccer, volleyball, and football games. A random act of kindness has created friendships.

"Eighty guys have gained a little sister forever," Lisa said. "She's formed such a bond with these people because they're real."

Their kindness has reaffirmed Lexi's efforts to give back. With the help of supporters, she's raised more than $110,000 for childhood cancer research for St. Baldrick's Foundation. Lexi knows the value of kindness. "That's just one way I can give back or help give back to everyone else," she said.

That effort matters, said Lisa, despite the unknowns. "We don't have any idea what's going to happen," she said.

"We live every single day. We don't go home and curl up in a ball and give up. She's not ready. I'm not ready for her to go."

So Lexi stays busy attending UCLA sporting events as a guest of athletes or students. She's also spent a lot of time with UCLA students who call her weekly to stay connected.

This, even more than that first pizza delivery, has meant a lot to Lexi.

She still has a battle ahead—but having friends makes a marked difference. "It makes it a lot easier because they give me things to do," Lexi said. "When I'm with them, I don't have to think about chemo. It's been so cool because I've gotten to meet a bunch of new people. Friends."

Kevin said the fraternity isn't going anywhere. They'll be a constant for Lexi. "We love her," he admits. "We'll be there for her forever."

✍

"The best way to find yourself is to lose yourself in the service of others." –Mahatma Gandhi

Great-Grandma Delivers Free Lunches to Needy Kids

"We are going out to these houses to deliver hope, love, and a lunch..."

THE VOLUNTEERS WHO work with Phyllis Shaughnessy call her "Saint Phyllis."

The kids who wait for her at the end of their driveways during the summer simply call her "the lunch lady."

That makes seventy-five-year-old Phyllis smile.

A year ago, she went looking for every child living within the boundaries of the North Beach School District who might be in need of a summer lunch. In northwestern Washington, that's a tall order. The coastal area is largely rural, and many families live tucked away down windy gravel roads. The houses can be hard to find, but Phyllis was on a mission.

"I got in my car and went all around, up and down every road, looking for evidence of kids," she said. "Out here, how else are you going to do it?"

That's how it began, the Green Lantern Lunches program, named after the local restaurant where the effort got its start. That summer, Phyllis and a handful of volunteers delivered more than fifteen thousand sack lunches to children who might otherwise have struggled to get a midday meal. Her program accomplished what government programs couldn't. It also sent a clear message: someone cares about you.

"We are going out to these houses to deliver hope, love, and a lunch to all the kids out here in the middle of nowhere," Phyllis said. "You get to know them. They'll tell you if they're having a good day or a bad day. You bridge the gap."

Solving a Problem

Government-funded summer lunch programs work in some places. In urban areas, children often can walk to a park or church where those lunches are distributed, but north of Ocean Shores, Washington, the population is too spread out. The nearest program closed because many children couldn't get to the church where it was offered, and regulations didn't allow for home delivery of the meals.

"It doesn't work," Phyllis said. "It didn't work."

A grandmother and retired postmaster, Phyllis knew there were rural kids in need. The small communities around her home in Copalis Beach aren't wealthy, and many families struggle to make ends meet. During the school year, they benefit from free or reduced-price lunches, but in the summer?

"They'd just make do," Phyllis said. "They might have to choose between having enough money for bread or milk."

So Phyllis solved the problem herself. She partnered with Green Lantern Tavern, a pub down the road from her house. Its owners agreed to let her use their kitchen to assemble lunches early in the morning before the breakfast crowd arrived.

A small team of volunteers stepped up to help her, gathering at the Green Lantern at 6:30 a.m. Monday through Friday to pack sacks with nonperishable foods such as boxes of macaroni and cheese, granola bars, chips, and cookies.

"We were going on a wing and a prayer," Phyllis said.

But donations came in from area residents. The money

kept the white paper lunch bags filled and the children who needed them fed all summer.

Volunteers followed Phyllis's lead, meeting kids in their driveway or at their front door.

"Is there anything you need?" she often asks them when she visits. "Can I help in any way?"

The face-to-face exchange is, in many ways, just as important as the food she brings.

"In order for them to establish respect for themselves, to realize they're important, they need to know that someone cares," Phyllis said. "This helps them make it through the week, and the kids know they're going to get their lunches."

"Do What You Can"

The first summer, the group delivered more than ten thousand lunches, about a hundred a day. The following year, Phyllis's route was thirty-eight miles round trip, with about fifty stops. By then, the children she visited watched and waited for her.

"They were so excited," she said. "They just jumped up and down when they saw the car. Their parents were really happy. It was a win-win situation."

That second summer, volunteers stopped assembling lunches at the Green Lantern, though the program's name remains the same. Now the group works out of the garage at Phyllis's home. And the workload has increased: the one hundred daily lunches have more than tripled to approximately 350.

Ed and Margaret Tegenfeldt have helped Phyllis since the program started. They deliver about a hundred lunches a day to children as young as two and as old as eighteen.

"There's a lot of joy in being able to make a difference in somebody else's life," Margaret said. "I think that's what we're in this world to do, to help others."

The retired couple is loyal to the program and to Phyllis, whom they credit for its success. "Phyllis has a heart for anyone in need," Ed said. "Anytime she can help someone, she's there."

Her dedication to children has prompted a great deal of media exposure—Green Lantern Lunch Program has been featured in national and local publications—and donations have followed. Some are relatively small, perhaps twenty or thirty dollars, while others are major contributions from companies from around the country.

Although Phyllis is grateful for the attention because it's kept the program going, she shies away from personal praise. "Do what you can," she said. "I think it was the way I was brought up. I was brought up to believe in helping people. It's so simple. What would you do if you knew there were children in the way-gone corners that no one was helping to feed?"

Phyllis makes it a point to talk with parents who are home when she delivers meals. Many of them appreciate a listening ear, and she's glad to offer it. "It's a feeling that you've done everything you can to make it a better day."

She even takes her seven-year-old grandson Nation along with her to make deliveries. "He says, 'Some kids need a lunch and we're going to bring it,'" she said. "It's a lesson in real life. To me it's just a way of life, to have that intention with people. They feel better for it and so do I."

"If you could only sense how important you are to the lives of those you meet; how important you can be to the people you may never even dream of." —Fred Rogers

Boy Gives up Birthday Party
to Honor Police Officers

WEARING A BIG smile and a perfectly tailored police uniform, Jeremie Bordua answered the door to his family's home. His pants were creased down the front, his light blue button-down shirt adorned with the same badge worn by Lansing Police Department officers. The hat atop his head bore the same emblem as theirs, with Michigan's state capitol in the center.

It all looked very official—because it was.

But Jeremie was just eleven years old.

In front of several hundred law enforcement officers, he had taken an oath to join their honorary ranks:

"I, Jeremie Bordua, hereby promise never to betray my badge, my integrity, and my character. I will always have the courage to hold myself and others accountable for our actions. I do solemnly affirm that I will always uphold the values of the law enforcement profession and that I will faithfully uphold the responsibilities of an honorary police officer, according to the best of my ability."

At the bottom of his signed oath, there are two signatures: Jeremie's and Lansing Police Chief Michael Yankowski's.

Jeremie's relationship with police has the humblest of beginnings. It started with a simple desire to say thank you. It was followed by national attention and praise, and resulted in friendships between a fifth grader struggling to overcome bullying and police officers all over the country who were grateful beyond measure for his unwavering kindness.

A Thank-You Party

Jeremie's eyes were filled with tears when his mom, Marcella Telling, picked him up after school one day. Fellow students were threatening to hurt him, he told her, and several of them had chased him on the playground.

"He hid under the playground equipment, crying and begging them to leave him alone," Marcella said.

The students who led the chase were suspended from school for a few days, but their actions changed Jeremie.

He was afraid.

A few weeks later, he saw a news segment on television.

The story about police brutality and misconduct concerned him, especially since he had dreamed of becoming a police officer since kindergarten.

"Mom, are they still good?" he asked. "Are police still the good guys?"

"I explained to him, just like every profession, there's good and there's bad, you know?" Marcella said. "But most of them are still the good guys."

"Some very bad things were being said about police officers," Jeremie said.

He wondered if there was any difference between the name-calling they were facing and what he'd endured on the playground. "I put myself into their place," he said.

And that's when he decided to do something.

"I believe in the police," Jeremie explained. "I wanted to put a smile on their face and make them happier about their job."

So he asked Marcella if his family could throw a police thank-you party. "We started talking about costs, and I said, 'Jeremie, it's going to be expensive,'" she said. "He looked at me and said, 'Well, Mom, for birthdays you always throw big birthday parties. Just use the money for my birthday for it.'

"I said, 'Do you know what that means?' He said, 'Yeah, I'm not going to have a birthday party.'"

"It Was Genuine"

Marcella said Jeremie was trying to create a positive outcome in the midst of controversy. "We just kinda went with it," she said. "If it was something he wanted to do, then we were going to find a way to do it."

Jeremie knew his mom liked to bake, so he suggested they sell her cookies to help pay for the party. They started a Facebook page titled "Jeremie's Cookies for a Cause."

"At first it just started off with our family and friends," Marcella said. "We didn't think it was going to get very far."

But their friends and family shared the page with other people. Word spread, and a local TV news producer caught wind of it and aired a story about Jeremie's plan for a police thank-you party.

Cookie orders went through the roof. Nearly five thousand cookies. That's how many sweet treats Marcella baked. "There were days I was doing seventy dozen cookies in a day," she said. "With three hours of sleep a night."

Officers and their families from all over mid-Michigan placed orders. Police departments in the area reached out and offered Jeremie tours of their facilities. They even stopped by his home to shake his hand and express their gratitude. "What you're doing means more to us than you'll ever know," they told him.

They also offered to help plan the party. Jeremie

toured several police departments, local jails, and dispatch centers. He met countless officers, all while continuing to raise money.

"It was a very busy summer," Marcella said. "Jeremie was making friends throughout all the different departments."

Thirty-year-old Ryan Smith is one of them. He's been a Lansing officer for a decade and said police have battled a negative national perception lately.

"People say, 'Heads up. Don't shoot' to me on the street," Ryan said. "It's hard to be out there doing your job if you're worried that people are going to second-guess you. I want people to realize we're professionals. We do this job to help people and give back to our community."

Jeremie's gesture was "shocking" at first, he said. "This is a little kid. He doesn't totally grasp what's going on with police right now, but he's going out of his way to thank police officers. It was genuine."

Friends for Life

By the time Jeremie's family held the party, his story had become national news. Two days before his eleventh birthday, more than two hundred uniformed men and women filled Eastern High School's field house for the long-awaited celebration. Among the local officers were police from as far away as Los Angeles and Georgia.

They ate treats, met with Jeremie, shook his hand, gave him heartfelt thank-yous, and posed for pictures. Because they knew about Jeremie's upcoming birthday, they also brought gifts, including a uniform and badge and several banners with the signature of nearly every police officer there, as well as a few paw prints from police dogs at various departments.

The banner messages are heartfelt.

"You're the man. Stay the way you are."

"Thank you for being so kind and thoughtful."

"We wish there were more people like you. Keep it up. You will go far in life."

The party brought tears to Marcella's eyes. "He's got friends for life," she said.

Jeremie ended up raising $10,000 through cookie sales, but because nearly everything at the party was donated, his family gave the money to a local holiday program in which police officers shop with needy children for gifts at Christmastime.

Jeremie said the party was a huge success. "I just know that now the officers have a smile on their faces," he said.

He's smiling more these days too.

After the party, he joined the Lansing Police Department in the Polar Plunge, jumping into freezing waters with several officers to raise money for athletes competing in the Special Olympics. He visited the Chicago Police Department and attended a Bulls' game with their officers, and he also traveled to Mississippi to meet police officers there.

He's an honor roll student now, something he'd never been before. "Ever since the party, nobody has bullied me," Jeremie said. "People want autographs and stuff."

Marcella said the family still receives messages from police officers across the country who want to thank Jeremie, and she's still selling cookies. They'll use the money to throw an annual barbecue for local police officers.

Ryan said the most rewarding outcome of Jeremie's kindness has been watching him gain the confidence he needed. "He knows he can become whatever he wants," he said. "And he basically has two hundred friends in the Lansing Police Department now."

Jeremie said his plans haven't changed. "I've always wanted to be a police officer ever since I was a little kid. They're brave and stuff, like me."

"Three things in human life are important: the first is to be kind; the second is to be kind; and the third is to be kind." –Henry James

Teen Wants to Change the World Through Inventions

"I'm not in it for anything but
to make the world a better
place, to inspire the world."

MAX LOUGHAN IS only thirteen, but don't underestimate him.

When he was four, he took everything apart that he could, piece by piece, including speakers, walkie-talkies, and radios. He needed to understand how they worked.

At age six, he earned a solid reputation as the neighborhood kid who could fix anyone's broken toy. By seven, Max began to invent things: a simple explosive device that detonated in his parents' garage, harmless and fun, and a wireless Morse code transmission device that worked underwater.

But at nine, Max made a decision. "If you make a difference, you change lives," he said. "I believe people should go out there and invent a better future. From that point on, I decided that's what I was going to do."

Max's goal is daunting: he wants to change the world.

And if his résumé so far is any indication, he probably will.

Meet Max

"Hi. My name is Max Loughan, and this is a short video about me. So let's get started."

His blond hair is combed back, away from his face, and he's wearing a white lab coat over his striped polo shirt. He opens the door to a small boiler room in his family's Nevada home and announces, "Welcome to my laboratory."

In the video Max uploaded to his YouTube channel, the camera pans amid the humming of pipes that run along the walls. Behind him is a computer, along with two chalkboards with scribbled calculations and diagrams.

In his spare time, he designs things—such as a fusion engine and a "real rocket engine" to power a boat across the lake near his home. He also takes online courses through Massachusetts Institute of Technology.

His inventions have given way to the creation of a device that has the potential to harvest electromagnetic energy. Using a coffee-can frame, wire, coils, tape, gum, and a spoon, Max captured energy for less than fifteen dollars. It might sound simple, but when he explains the device, you realize it isn't.

"The invention's potential to provide energy to economically disadvantaged people and communities could be life changing," he said. "Imagine electricity reaching rural corners of the globe where residents have very little means to afford it."

According to Max, this is only the beginning. "My goal is not to get money or gain fame or anything. I'm not in it for anything but to make the world a better place, to inspire the world. The world could be a better place. It can be, so why shouldn't it be?"

A Thoughtful Approach

Mary Loughan won't deny that her son is gifted. But what she loves about him is the thoughtful way he approaches the world. A neighbor once dubbed her son "an old soul." She believes there's truth to that.

In fourth grade, Max spent about ten months as a

vegetarian. "He decided that's how he was going to do his part to change the world," Mary said.

Then he began inventing things. "Mom, I need to come up with something that's going to change the world," he'd tell her. "What do you need right now, every day?"

This question says a lot about him, according to Mary. "I think he tries to explain things to me to help me see things differently. He's thirteen years old and has only thirteen years of experience, but he's trying to make me look at things differently."

"I Can't Even Imagine"

Not everything Max invents is potentially world changing. Some of it's just for fun. He is a kid, after all.

For instance, he's working on a "laser saber" or light-saber, which, when he's finished, will cut through paper or cardboard. Then there's a guitar he's making, which eventually will create music by shooting vibrations into the air.

The work is trial and error, and nothing comes easy. "My stuff fails all the time," Max confessed. "When you invent something, at first it fails."

The key, according to Max, is never giving up on an idea. "I just don't leave them," he said. "I find a way around them. Once I start something, I finish it."

Mary said her son's dedication has convinced her he

has a bright future. "I do believe he's going to change the world. I don't know how and I don't know when, but he will."

When asked what he'll be inventing when he's eighteen, Max was honest. "I can't even imagine," he said.

But he does believe it will be something that could make people's lives better and easier. Something good. "Bad things come and go," he said, "but good events can last forever."

&

"Goodness is the only investment that never fails." –Henry David Thoreau.

FINDING PURPOSE THROUGH KINDNESS

One-Hundred-Year-Old
Makes a Dress Every Day

THE BEAUTY OF Lillian Weber's work is in the details.

Shiny, colorful buttons; lace trim; and carefully sewn pockets. They're embellishments she often adds to the dresses she makes for young girls who live half a world away.

Every day, for more than four years, she's sat at her sewing machine in Bettendorf, Iowa, piecing together bright fabrics a few hours at a time. The finished dresses hang on a rack in her farmhouse.

Lillian has made more than 1,200 of them. That's at least one dress a day.

She's made it her mission to help clothe youngsters in need by donating them to a Michigan-based nonprofit called Little Dresses for Africa.

Not bad for a one-hundred-year-old mother of five.

Always Positive, Always Busy

Lillian has been sewing since she was eight years old. She learned in 4-H, made her own clothes for years, and eventually sewed outfits for her children and grandchildren.

"Most of the clothes we had were handmade, and then, when we had children, she was always making them dresses," one of her daughters, LeAnn, said.

Lillian's husband Frank was a foreman at a tractor plant. According to LeAnn, her parents were a self-sufficient couple: the family grew up on a forty-acre farm where they churned their own butter, harvested corn and alfalfa, and raised cattle and chickens.

Lillian was an active stay-at-home mom with a kind word for everyone she met. "If you saw the term 'great mom' in the dictionary, you'd see a picture of our mom there," LeAnn said. "She's always positive, always friendly."

To Lillian, movement is part of life. When LeAnn was growing up, her mother loved to bake, never missed church on Sunday, and tended to everything in the huge garden on their property.

"She needs to be busy," LeAnn said. "She's not content if she's not. I think she feels like if she's not busy she's wasting her life."

After nearly seventy years of marriage, Frank passed away. Activities that had been a source of joy for

Lillian—such as baking and gardening—became difficult for her.

Then Little Dresses for Africa gave her what she desperately needed: purpose.

Finding Purpose

"I want to be a part of this," Lillian told LeAnn one day.

She handed her an article clipping about a group of local women who volunteered with Little Dresses for Africa. Using a simple pattern, they were sewing dresses for the organization to send overseas to children in impoverished countries.

"We should call them," Lillian said.

So they did. A meeting was arranged, and Lillian joined the effort from home.

"This was a godsend," LeAnn said. "When she started doing this, it was what she needed. She was immediately content."

That was the start of Lillian's grand undertaking.

Every morning she woke up, made her bed, ate breakfast, and sewed. The dresses were bright; each one unique, careful creations with Lillian's signature details. LeAnn and her sisters, Linda and Sherry, often helped by sorting fabric and cutting it for Lillian, who'd praise the inventory from her seat at the sewing machine.

"Oh, that fabric's so pretty," she'd remark.

"That's my favorite color."

"I can't wait to see how this one turns out."

The number of finished dresses climbed—five to six new ones a week—and her pace rarely slowed. As the garments made their way to Michigan, then overseas, Lillian and her daughters kept a running tally of the inventory. The total ticked upward to three hundred, six hundred, nine hundred. One day Lillian set a new goal: one thousand dresses by her one hundredth birthday.

Devoted to the Cause

It was a quiet declaration until a local television station caught wind of what Lillian was doing. "When that got out, that's when it went viral," LeAnn said.

National media covered the story.

The world responded.

Lillian received 850 birthday cards.

A reporter also reached out to Little Dresses for Africa's founder, Rachel O'Neill, who started the nonprofit in 2008 after taking a trip to Africa. Her efforts have resulted in five million dresses for needy girls in eighty-three countries. The dresses are a source of comfort and protection for many of the recipients. According to Rachel, the girls who wear them often see them as a symbol of hope, a reminder that they're worthy of respect and safety.

"Anyone that needs them, we say yes to," Rachel said. "The children that receive them have very little."

Although she'd never met Lillian, her story instantly touched her. "Lillian was quoted as saying, 'I know I'll probably never see my dresses on a little girl,'" Rachel said. The statement struck Rachel. She wanted Lillian to see the difference she was making in so many girls' lives.

At Lillian's hundredth birthday party, Rachel showed up with photos from a recent trip to Africa. In them, girls stood smiling for the camera, clad in Lillian's creations.

"Mom just cried when she saw that," LeAnn said.

The two women embraced and became fast friends. "She's precious," Rachel said. "Absolutely precious. Anyone who meets a milestone like that on their one hundredth birthday is special."

LeAnn said her mother takes pride in the accomplishment. "She thinks it's great. It gives her so much pride to know she's helping these little girls."

Rachel thinks Lillian serves as proof that no one is ever too old to make a difference in the world. "It's the whole idea that you still have value regardless of your age," she said. "Lillian represents so many people."

LeAnn agreed. "Just because you're older doesn't mean

you shouldn't be doing something. Mom says, 'Other than the fact that I can't do all that I once did, I don't feel one hundred.'"

LeAnn credits Little Dresses for Africa for that. It might help others, but it saved Lillian. "If Mom wasn't making these dresses," she said, "she wouldn't be here today. I know that."

"I think a hero is any person really intent on making this a better place for all people." –Maya Angelou

A Sense of Home

"You make someone happy, but you're also giving meaning to your own life because you're really making a difference."

"I'VE GOT MY first apartment," the message read. "Can you help me?"

The note was sent to Georgie Smith through her interior design and entertaining website, "Georgie Smith Home."

Georgie agreed to meet the young man at his apartment in Long Beach, California, his first home outside the foster care system in which he'd been raised. There, the Australian-born film producer, designer, and chef came face-to-face with what many foster youth encounter when they turn eighteen.

It was an unforgettable visit. As Georgie walked into the complex, she heard tenants yelling behind closed doors in various apartments. "It was dark and depressing," she said. "He had a bunk bed with an old mattress, and everything else was in plastic bags. I thought, *Well, that's not right.* It was up to me. I saw a problem; I saw a solution, so I did something about it."

After soliciting donations of furniture and household goods from friends and contacts, Georgie turned the cold, drab apartment into a home.

The gesture sparked a movement.

Georgie and her partner Melissa Goddard started a nonprofit dedicated to giving real homes to young men and women who leave the foster care system. They call it A Sense of Home.

"It Felt Like a Family"

Imagine moving into your first apartment with garbage bags instead of suitcases, a sleeping bag instead of a bed— and no support system to help you create a home within the four walls you find yourself in.

For youth who age out of the foster care system, "home" can be a difficult concept to grasp. "When you don't have family, you don't have community, and community is what opens up opportunity," Georgie said. "That's what community does, and they don't have that."

Yolanda Elam didn't know what community was before A Sense of Home helped her. The former foster-care youth turned to the organization after she signed a lease on her first apartment, a small studio. Yolanda was sleeping on the floor, and what little she owned was stored in boxes next to where she slept, her clothing neatly folded in piles against the wall.

A Sense of Home staff and volunteers brought her furniture, necessities, and decorations. They organized the space, played music, brought food, and celebrated with Yolanda, holding a housewarming in her transformed apartment.

"Everyone sat around and we all talked," Yolanda said. "Everyone shared. I shared my story. I've never had anything like that, people who cared about me. It felt like a family. It was something special. It wasn't just one person coming in to help me. It was a group of people, and they weren't a group of social workers. They weren't paid to do it. It was a group of people who came together to say I mattered. I never really thought there were people like that."

"I Was So Lost"

Thirty-year-old Loren Elam is the operations manager at A Sense of Home's inventory warehouse in Venice, California.

She oversees the donated furniture and other items that will fill the apartments of young men and women who've left the foster-care system in the Los Angeles area.

The work is very close to her heart. Fifteen years ago, Loren ran away from an abusive home and was placed in foster care herself. She bounced from placement to placement, attending seven different high schools.

At age eighteen, "I just got the boot," she said. "When you age out of the foster-care system, you kind of go into panic mode. You have no clue what you're going to do."

For her that meant living in a small apartment with roommates. As she didn't have a car or bike, a trip to the grocery store was a two-hour trek on foot.

When Loren couldn't pay her rent, she left and ended up homeless. She slept in a park for four months. Then she started using drugs. When it rained, she spent her nights in abandoned buildings, watching other addicts use drugs and sometimes overdose.

"I was so lost," she said. "I didn't know what to do."

Then she secured a job, and a purpose, with A Sense of Home. "They just accepted me with open arms. It has been a long journey; I feel like I'm almost sixty."

Loren has aligned herself with an organization that provides the kind of support she was missing twelve years earlier.

A Close-Knit Community

A Sense of Home's clients receive new furniture and home goods for their new apartments, what Georgie calls "inspired spaces," designed to feel welcoming—but they also become part of a close-knit community the nonprofit has created.

People who volunteer include community members who want to help, as well as former foster-care kids who aged out of the system, benefited from A Sense of Home's generosity, and show up to pay it forward.

When A Sense of Home gathers to furnish a space, staff and volunteers carry a couch, dressers, chairs, and beds into empty rooms. They decorate the space within a few hours and hold a housewarming party for the recipient. The gatherings include stories from former foster-care youth about their experiences.

"Everybody has tears in their eyes," said Barbara Thornburg, a volunteer and writer who takes part in move-in efforts and housewarmings whenever she can. "It's an amazing organization. When you help someone else, you get so much back. I love it because it's so one-on-one. You're not just writing a check; you get more than that. You make someone happy, but you're also giving meaning to your own life because you're really making a difference. That makes you feel good all day."

The stories people share at the housewarming parties

bring peace to those who tell them and inspire those who listen. "It's a beautiful, hopeful way to tell their story," Georgie said. "It's so beautiful and pure and cathartic."

"Where You're at Your Best"

A Sense of Home has helped more than 180 people and furnished more than 150 homes for Los Angeles–area residents between the ages of nineteen and twenty-eight. This is done with a handful of paid staff and help from many volunteers.

Georgie hopes to grow the organization by setting up chapters outside of California. She receives many inquiries from people around the country who are interested in helping her make that happen.

"I think when you're really in service to others, nothing else matters in life," she said. "Showing up and being good to others at all times is really where you're at your best."

A Sense of Home has given her something nothing else could, she said. "It's a humanity thing. You get high on humanity, and I think what we want in life is to be connected to others."

Caring About Others Together

When Loren was at the lowest point in her life—resigned to sleeping in a park every night because she didn't have a home—she felt worthless. Now she knows she's showing other foster-care youth that someone cares about them. "We can't control the things that have happened in our past," she said, "but we can control our future." Loren said she lives by that saying now. "I always felt like there should be something more after foster care to help these kids. Now there is."

A Sense of Home also forever changed how Yolanda looks at the world. Today she's the organization's program director. In the years since the group furnished her first apartment, she's helped throw more than two hundred housewarmings. Each one is special, she said, and proof that good is alive and well.

"Nowadays, with what's going on in the world, this is what it looks like when people care about each other."

"A single act of kindness throws out roots in all directions, and the roots spring up and make new trees." —Amelia Earhart

One Woman's Quest to Save an Entire Dog Shelter

WHY DEVOTE YOURSELF to saving more than two hundred abused and neglected dogs from a run-down animal shelter thousands of miles away?

Although people have asked thirty-two-year-old Danielle Eden-Scheinberg this question countless times, she always struggles with giving a concrete answer.

"I feel like I came to this world for a reason," she said. "I'm trying to save as many [animals] as I can."

She's been making good on that goal for two years as the co-owner of Dog Tales Rescue and Sanctuary, a massive shelter on fifty acres in King City, Ontario.

Danielle and her husband Rob live on the former horse farm with more than a hundred rescued dogs and seventy horses. Their staff of forty-five also cares for rescued cows, pigs, ducks, and rabbits.

An actress by trade, Danielle is constantly on the lookout for more animals in need. During a visit to central Israel, where she grew up, she was confronted with a heartbreaking situation: 270 dogs trapped in a cramped, dirty shelter near Kidron, about a half hour south of Tel Aviv.

Most of the dogs had skin that was infected, blotchy, and red. The animals were infested with fleas and neglected, fighting over scraps of rotten meat and bread.

"It smelled like death," Danielle said. "I had to turn around and walk back out at first."

In that moment, she made a decision.

"I told the lady, 'I'll take the entire shelter.'"

A Simple Message

It's a daunting task, saving 270 dogs from deplorable conditions. You have to nurse each one back to health, show them how to live life outside the muddy cage they've occupied for years, then nudge them toward trusting humans again, Danielle said.

Then you have to try and find them the right adoptive family.

Danielle said it took her only seconds to make the decision to save these dogs. "I kind of looked at it, and I said, 'How do I do it? Where do I start?' It doesn't matter... the situation of those dogs or how bad they were, we were going to bring them here. Once I make a commitment, I make a commitment."

Danielle's staff was shocked when they learned about her intention to save so many dogs from so far away, but only for "about five seconds," said Clare Forndran, who had been working at Dog Tales for more than a year. "Then we thought, *That's just like Danielle.* It's the typical project at Dog Tales. We do things on a huge scale on a regular basis."

The staff at Dog Tales has adopted out more than seven hundred dogs from Canada and the US since the rescue organization was founded in 2014. The shelter also bids on horses that are auctioned off for slaughter, purchases them, and gives them a permanent home on its property.

Their message is simple, Clare said: rescue dogs deserve our love and compassion. "Sadly we live in a disposable society. People see animals as a product or as food before they see them as a life. I really do feel like we're changing perceptions."

But the dogs Danielle vowed to save from the shelter in Israel were some of the worst cases of neglect and abuse her staff had ever seen. Danielle began moving them out of the Kidron shelter in batches and established a smaller shelter in Israel, where a vet examined each one. "There was one dog that couldn't even stand up; he had been there for so long," Danielle said.

After the dogs were examined and treated, she moved them to foster homes near the shelter. Once they were well enough to travel a long distance, she transported them—a few at a time—to her shelter in Ontario. There the staff immediately embraced the task of showing them kindness and love.

"When the dogs first arrived, they were so shut down," Clare said. "We just spent hours in the rooms with them, helping them to be comfortable with people. There's so much love for these dogs."

It took months to build connections, to teach the dogs how to walk on leashes and interact with humans.

The sanctuary's staff wrote about the endeavor on their website and Facebook page, and Danielle often tells the story. "People need to know about it," she said. "I'm pretty sure other people would have done what I did if they could."

The Right Homes

In the months since Danielle assumed responsibility for the Kidron shelter's population, nearly all the dogs have been rescued. Some didn't survive, while others are still being transferred to the sanctuary in Ontario.

"People who adopt these dogs, they know it's a project," she said. "Many people are looking for the dogs who will wag their tail and look them in the eyes. Not all of these dogs will do that."

Danielle meets every prospective adoptive family, some who travel hours just to see the animals. "I want to meet the families," she said. "I want to make sure they go to the right home."

Although helping the dogs find real homes is at the core of the organization's effort, seeing them off is bittersweet. "They usually open up pretty quickly, and once they do, it doesn't take long to find them homes," Clare said. "Honestly, it's a roller coaster of emotions."

And finding loving homes for abused and neglected dogs is truly rewarding. "I'm attached to all of them," Danielle said. "I really am. I rescued them myself, one by one. I'm happy because I gave them a new life. That's my goal."

✍

"We make a living by what we get, but we make a life by what we give." –Winston Churchill

Farmer Gives Away Harvest

EVERY ONION, MELON, tomato, ear of sweet corn, string bean, zucchini, and cucumber growing in the earth at Jonathan Lawler's thirty-six-acre farm is spoken for.

The produce won't be sold to wholesalers. You won't find it on grocery store shelves or at a farmers' market.

Instead, the half million pounds of food expected during the first harvest season at Brandywine Creek Farms in Greenfield, Indiana, is intended for soup kitchens and food banks throughout the state.

This bounty will feed hundreds of poverty-stricken people. And next year, Jonathan, a husband and a father to three boys, will plant and grow even more to give away.

The thirty-nine-year-old farmer had decided to take a year off from farming. But he quickly changed his mind when his fifteen-year-old son, Gabriel, told him about all the hungry kids at his school in rural Indiana.

Sometimes when your eyes are opened to a need, it's impossible to shut them again, Jonathan said. "I'll be damned if I'll let a kid in my county go hungry. We have to help our neighbors."

Hungry Neighbors

The Lawler farm is fourteen miles from Indianapolis. It's a sprawling property, home to bald eagles, deer, and a variety of other wildlife. The family bought it in 2009 and farmed there until 2015. The previous year had been hard, though. Crops were scarce and harvesting difficult.

"I had the worst year I've ever had in farming," Jonathan said.

So he decided to take a break from working the fields and landed a job in human resources for a large trucking firm.

Then one day Jonathan and Gabriel were walking the property, scouting spots for their upcoming deer-hunting season. Walking along, enjoying each other's company and deep in conversation, Gabriel asked if they'd be able to donate some of the venison to his school's food pantry.

Jonathan stopped in his tracks, shocked by the notion that some of his son's classmates were going hungry. "What are you talking about?" he asked him.

"My idea of somebody who was hungry was a person

sleeping under a bridge in Indianapolis," Jonathan said. "That's what I thought hungry people were. That was not my community. That was not my county."

But rural poverty existed nearby.

Jonathan learned that poor families in Gabriel's school district were dependent on food pantries in the area, including the one at his son's school. Many of them lacked transportation or opportunities to find food elsewhere.

"The more people I talked to, the more I found out," Jonathan said. "There are hungry kids going to school in my county."

He found himself looking out at the acres surrounding his home. He knew he could grow plenty of food on the land—food that was good for people, food that was desperately needed.

Produce in grocery stores can be pricey. And in food banks and soup kitchens, it's hard to come by, rarely donated because of its limited shelf life.

So Jonathan and his wife Amanda had a heart-to-heart.

"You leave my farm and drive to my son's school, and all you do is pass other farms, but there were still all these hungry kids," he said.

Jonathan and Amanda imagined struggling to feed their children and decided it was a reality others shouldn't have to live with. "This is not something these people have the ability to do, and we could help," he said. "I could offer them wholesome food that would help them."

Farm on a Mission

Jonathan decided to take on a new kind of farming. This year's harvest isn't for profit; it's for the betterment of others. "This is not about making money off farming," he said. "This is about helping people."

Brandywine Creek Farms is on a mission.

"We're shaping beds and getting ready to plant now," Jonathan said in the spring.

Onions are already in the ground, and melons will be soon, but the biggest crop will likely be tomatoes. Jonathan is expecting to grow 250,000 pounds of them this season. When they're ripe, they'll be donated to area food banks to be given away as needed.

The farm already has sponsorship from a local hospital, and it also has volunteers, including a few at-risk youth who spend time working the land there.

Jonathan has plans for the farm, which has since become a nonprofit. Eventually he would like it to be self-sustaining. He wants to set aside acreage for growing produce he'll sell wholesale, in hopes that those profits will pay for the production of an estimated 600,000 pounds of donated food.

"It's like a gigantic community garden," he said. "Imagine it that way."

Jonathan hopes other Indiana farms join the effort, setting aside a portion of their crops for the needy. In a leap of faith, he's completely committed himself to the effort. He left his human resources position with the trucking company and happily returned to full-time farming.

"I Feel Such Peace"

"I go out into the fields," he said. "And these fields are everything. My blood, my sweat, and my tears are in these fields. If my donation can help my neighbors, if I can do that, I'm going to do that."

The change agrees with him wholeheartedly. Amanda recently told Jonathan he's the happiest she's ever seen him. He even sleeps better now, she said.

Opening one's eyes and giving back can have a healing effect on the giver. "I feel such peace in doing this," he said. "It's the least amount of money I've ever made in my life, but I'm also the most joyous I've ever been."

❧

"The generous will themselves be blessed, for they share their food with the poor." –Proverbs 22:9

Car Wash Changes Lives of People with Autism

JOHN D'ERI AND his son, Thomas, wouldn't be in the car wash business if it weren't for their youngest family member, Andrew.

Andrew works at the business they started, Rising Tide Car Wash, carefully cleaning and waxing vehicle exteriors, alongside coworkers he has something in common with: autism.

Eighty percent of the staff are on the autism spectrum. Most, like Andrew, have a cognitive impairment. The job is often a first for these employees, most of whom fall in the middle of the spectrum.

Their mission is simple, Thomas said. "Here we like the idea of helping people grow."

Rising Tide Car Wash opened in South Florida in 2013. The operation includes two locations and employs about eighty people. On any given day, its hard work welcoming people and washing cars.

Because of Andrew

John and Thomas work with special education teachers and staff at local school districts and transitional education programs in their community to recruit staff who have autism and are looking for employment. Today, Rising Tide Car Wash's staff washes more than 150,000 cars a year.

Andrew and other employees who fall in the middle of the autism spectrum have flourished there. The work has given them a sense of purpose, a skill set, and confidence. They've made friends among the staff too.

The business's goal is to provide these individuals with opportunities and to change public perceptions regarding people living with autism. "Every person on the autism spectrum is different," Thomas explained. "It had to be about changing stereotypes because that was what held Andrew back."

Before Rising Tide opened, Thomas and his father met with educators, as well as individuals on the autism spectrum. "I wanted to meet as many people with autism as I could," Thomas said. He spoke with people who were detail oriented and conscientious about their work but who struggled socially. Although they learned differently, they were driven.

"They had some really strong skill sets," he said. Among them was a fierce work ethic and attention to details.

What Thomas and his father learned led them to start their car wash. They believed every one of these individuals deserved an opportunity, and they realized too many people don't see what those with autism have to offer.

Creating Bonds and Building Self Confidence

Nineteen-year-old Matt, a quality control team leader at Rising Tide Car Wash, is on the autism spectrum. "I like cleaning cars a lot," he said. "I achieve my goals here."

He isn't alone. For the approximately eighty individuals who work at the car wash's two locations, the job has become a means to independence and also a meaningful social outlet. Several of the business's employees are part of a tight-knit circle of friends.

"A lot of our employees we've had for a few years now," Thomas said. "They're building these much deeper social relationships. I think it's a large part of what makes this work." As a result, the car wash is a place where its employees want to be, and it shows in their work. "People are happy to be at work, to do their job," he added.

Matt is good friends with many of his coworkers, and at times they feel like a second family to him. "We have fun. We usually go out after work together too."

"Managers help foster those bonds," Thomas explained, "organizing regular social outings for staff outside work." For example, they take group trips to bowling alleys and restaurants. "To teach these guys and see them hanging out, that's what makes you feel it's worth it."

Brotherly Bond

Andrew fits right in among the automated car wash tunnels and interior cleaning stations at the family business. He works hard and continues to learn new skills.

"Because of it, Andrew has learned to try new things, to be more social," Thomas said.

Working together also has strengthened Andrew's relationship with his older brother. "We're closer now. I get to work with Andrew on a daily basis. I get to be a big part of his life."

Thomas says the business really makes a difference. "This is helping people grow as individuals. They have more self-confidence; they have income; they get to work toward a common goal, with peers—true peers—people who have the same life experience as they do."

It's one of the reasons Matt loves his job. "They're good to me and I'm good to them, and that's all that matters."

Opening and running Rising Tide Car Wash has been rewarding, Thomas said. "It can be really challenging to run any small business, but what makes it worth continuing through those challenges is the fact that you're changing the lives of the people who work for you."

"Never doubt that a small group of committed citizens can change the world. Indeed, it is the only thing that has." —Margaret Mead

CONNECTING TO OTHERS THROUGH KINDNESS

Disabled Veteran Receives an Unexpected Gift from a Secret Angel

---

"I hope this secret angel knows how amazing they are and how grateful our family is for their generosity!"

CHRISTOPHER GARRETT HAS a secret angel.

That's what his wife, Brittany, calls the person who ended Christopher's twice-weekly struggle to maintain their lawn.

The disabled US Army veteran took on the task every week, limping as he navigated the couple's push lawn mower around the property at a slow but steady pace. Mowing the front yard and backyard took him about four hours. He'd finish exhausted, sore, but determined to keep doing it.

"People would see me out there struggling," Christopher said.

Then an anonymous stranger gave the thirty-one-year-old a gift that made the task a joy—a brand-new John Deere riding lawn mower.

It was delivered to his house with a note: "I hope this saves time for the things that matter most in your life. Thank you for your service and for my freedom."

The note was signed, "A grateful American."

That morning, as Christopher stood at his front door, reading the words, tears streamed down his face. "I couldn't stop them," he said. "I couldn't believe it. It surprised me, because what I'd noticed is the world's getting darker."

All it took was one unexpected act of kindness to restore his faith in humanity.

An Honorable Discharge

Mowing the lawn is a point of pride for Christopher.

On June 29, 2011, he was four years into his enlistment and stationed in Afghanistan when his unit was tasked with a night patrol. They were walking down a road near a village when machine-gun fire erupted from twenty-five yards away. Christopher was hit. The bullet entered below his belly button, shattering his pelvis and clipping a major artery. He lay on the ground for forty-five minutes, bleeding internally, as his unit worked to rescue him while fending off gunfire.

He remembers very little about the helicopter ride to an area military base. When they landed, a chaplain clasped his hand and prayed over him.

"I could feel my heart beat slowing down," Christopher said. "I knew I was getting really close to dying."

He underwent three surgeries and a lifesaving blood transfusion before the army honorably discharged him in January 2013. "I had to learn how to walk again," he said.

These days, there's an inch missing from the pelvic area in his right hip. He's also suffered from some post-traumatic stress, but his physical challenges are a greater burden, he said. He walks with a limp and struggles with sitting upright.

"I'm very limited. Just going to the grocery store kills me. The pain's always in my right hip area."

The transition back to civilian life hasn't been easy. Christopher and Brittany live in Oregon, where they both grew up. They've raised their infant son Thomas there in the small community of Joseph. Brittany is a waitress at a café, and Christopher receives disability compensation.

Mowing the lawn with a push mower wasn't something

he looked forward to, but he wanted to do it even though it sometimes took him several hours to recover.

"To a normal person, it's probably like pushing a lawn mower, but for me it was like pushing a car," Christopher said.

Life-Changing Gift

A week before the new mower showed up, Christopher cut the grass with his push mower, stopping every few minutes to collect himself and rest his leg.

"It was really hard for me that day," he said.

Then one morning he answered a knock at the front door to find a deliveryman holding an envelope.

"He said, 'Could you help me unload something?'"

The riding mower in the back of the delivery truck retailed for more than $2,000.

Brittany broke down in tears when she saw it. "It was pretty intense that day," she said.

So intense that she posted a message on Facebook, hoping to reach the mysterious secret angel. "Something AMAZING happened today!" she wrote. "THANK YOU WHOEVER YOU ARE!!"

A week later, Christopher climbed into the driver's seat and cut the couple's lawn in less than twenty minutes.

Pain free and very grateful, he smiled for the photos Brittany later shared on Facebook.

"The smile on his face was my favorite," she wrote on the social media site. "He never smiled during this chore before! I hope this secret angel knows how amazing they are and how grateful our family is for their generosity!!! I will forever pray that God shower you and your family with blessings."

Christopher still wonders about the identity of his Good Samaritan. "We still have no idea," he said. Whoever it was, he hopes he or she knows how much this generous gift has helped him. "If I could, I would immediately thank them and tell them they have no idea how much it helped. The fact that they care about my suffering, that's the big thing to me."

He'll will never forget that. A stranger changed his perspective, he said, and he's better because of it. "They have a special place in my heart for the rest of my life."

⤡

"Generosity is the flower of justice." –Nathaniel Hawthorne

Football Team Surprises Teammate with a Secret Play

"I couldn't have felt happier
than that moment."

REMARKABLE FOOTBALL TOUCHDOWNS are a joy to watch.

They put points on the board and drive fans out of their seats and onto their feet. They're a thing of beauty, showcasing everything from amazing athleticism to teamwork and gutsy determination.

But a few years ago, households around the nation paid particular attention to a touchdown, courtesy of Olivet Middle School's Eagles, that took nearly everyone outside the team by surprise. The feat was captured on video: a group of eighth-grade boys surrounding teammate Keith Orr and ushering him over the goal line with the ball.

You can hear the crowd cheer as Keith scores. But that isn't why the video went viral. And it isn't why so many people praised the Eagles. The story behind their touchdown—the story of what it took to get Keith to the one-yard line and why the team wanted him there—deserves all the credit.

It's proof that a touchdown can showcase something else entirely: kindness.

"They Just Had His Back"

Whenever Keith describes the moment he crossed the goal line clutching a football to his chest, it still brings a smile to his face.

"It was indescribable," he said in his parents' living room at their farmhouse in rural Michigan.

He would graduate from high school soon and was taking auto mechanic classes at a career center, with hopes of using the skills he'd acquired fixing tractors and other machinery on his parents' farm.

But when Keith was in middle school, he needed a structured outlet, said Carrie Orr, his mother. He has attention deficit/hyperactivity disorder, is very strong willed, and struggles with maintaining personal boundaries.

Keith also knew nothing about football, but Carrie

and her husband, Jim, thought a team sport would be good for him, so they contacted the Eagles' organizers.

The twenty-member team welcomed him, and he attended his first practice. "He didn't know what a touchdown was," Carrie said. "They had to explain everything to him. He was so excited when he got home. He was like, 'I love it. I can't wait to go back.'"

Sheridan Hedrick, then thirteen and a running back on the team, said when Keith joined the team he was surprised—and he wasn't alone.

"Everyone was kind of talking about it at practice," Sheridan said. "I knew he had learning disabilities, and he wasn't physically built or anything."

Sheridan wondered if Keith would have trouble handling the physical demands of the sport. Would he be able to contribute during practices or games?

Keith surprised him. He showed up to every practice, helped coaches with drills, and became a valued member of the team, learning as the season progressed and lightening the mood with jokes.

The coaches supported and encouraged Keith, and his teammates befriended him. "He's never really had friends who included him," Carrie said. "He doesn't get invited to parties or over to people's houses."

The football team offered Keith something he'd been

missing. "They were like his brothers," she explained. "They wouldn't let anyone mess with him. They stood up for him. It was neat to watch how they encouraged him. They just had his back."

The Plan

After Keith joined the football team, Beth Hedrick, Sheridan's mother, said her son talked about him a lot. "Guess what Keith did today, Mom?" he'd tell her proudly on rides home from practice.

It was clear to her that the two boys were bonding, but Beth was surprised when, midway through the season, Sheridan told her he wanted to help Keith score a touchdown.

"They accepted him for who he was," Beth said. "They had a plan. They knew what they were going to do."

The idea started out simply, a whim, a what-if scenario everyone on the team supported.

"We always kind of talked about it like, 'What if we got Keith a touchdown? Yeah, that would be cool. That'd be sweet,'" Sheridan said. "He just enjoyed the sport so much, and we wanted to make him feel like he accomplished something, because he had."

Unbeknownst to Keith, the Eagles went to their coaches and told them about a play Sheridan had designed to get as close to the goal line as possible without scoring. If they could execute it with enough time on the clock to bring Keith on the field, they could usher him to the end zone.

It would take a team effort to pull off—and just the right circumstances.

While they were playing a game against Eaton Rapids, Sheridan saw the opportunity he'd been waiting for. The running back ran the ball as close to the goal line as he could, taking a knee just before scoring a touchdown, and before anyone in the stands could grasp what was happening, the coaches motioned for Keith to take to the field.

Sheridan handed him the ball; the game resumed; and the Eagles surrounded Keith. They ushered him into the end zone and to a touchdown. "We just pushed him in," Sheridan said.

Carrie and Jim were sitting in the stands when their friends yelled, "Watch! Watch!"

"We didn't expect it at all," she said.

The Eagles carried Keith off the field on their shoulders. In an essay Keith penned later that year in class, honoring Sheridan as his hero, he wrote, "I couldn't have felt happier than that moment."

Sheridan said Keith deserved that happiness. "He should get more recognition for being out there all the time. People like Keith struggle through a lot, so they just need to be treated like everyone else so they don't feel so different."

A Once-in-a-Lifetime Gesture

Keith's touchdown has been viewed millions of times online. Local and national news outlets have told the team's story, and in the year that followed, the Eagles were honored with the Harlem Globetrotters' Junior Phenom Award for caring enough to single Keith out.

Beth said the boys involved were just "a good, close group of kids," but what they did led to a once-in-a-lifetime opportunity for Keith. "People never get tired of hearing about it," she said. "People still bring it up. They still talk about it."

Carrie understands why. She still expresses disbelief over the fact that a group of teenagers carried out such a kind, selfless act. It isn't what you'd expect from middle-school boys, she said.

"Eighth graders don't do that," she remarked. "I just couldn't believe it. I heard from a lot of people who told me, 'Their story is wonderful. It restored my faith in humanity.' I think the country just needed a feel-good story."

For Keith, and Sheridan, it's easier to understand—and to sum up—as something good friends did for one of their own. "We cared about him," Sheridan said. "It felt really good."

Keith has never forgotten how it made him feel. "It was cool," he said. "It made it a good year."

∽

"Kindness, I've discovered, is everything in life." –Isaac Bashevis Singer

---

Teacher Gives Lifesaving Gift to Student

"It was relief. It was joy.
It was happiness."

NATASHA FULLER'S DAYS at Oakfield Elementary School in Wisconsin are pretty typical.

She goes to classes, plays with friends during recess, and trades laughs in the lunchroom with other students. These are everyday occurrences she can count on.

But no school day would be complete for nine-year-old Natasha without a hug from third-grade teacher Jodi Schmidt.

"I see her every day," Natasha said. "When I go to school, I see her in the hallway and I give her a hug and say, 'How is your day?' She's my favorite teacher."

Jodi's been teaching at the school for a decade, and lots of students know her, but she and Natasha have a special bond.

Jodi saved the girl's life.

Natasha had suffered from near renal failure since age two and was diagnosed with prune belly syndrome—also known as Eagle-Barrett syndrome—shortly after birth. Her abdominal muscles struggled to develop, and her kidneys suffered. At age eight, she had been on dialysis for five years and desperately needed a new kidney, but recurring infections and illness kept bumping her off the transplant list.

Then Jodi, a mother of three, donated one of her kidneys to Natasha. She said she was "pulled" to help the dainty girl with long blond hair.

The day Jodi found out her kidney was a match for Natasha was one of the best of her life. Some things are simply meant to be, she said. "I'd never felt so confident in any decision I've ever made."

A Gift

Natasha didn't know about Jodi's decision to donate a kidney to her until she was called to the principal's office one morning.

Before that, she'd struggled to live a normal life. Her

failing kidneys left her exhausted. She often lacked the energy to play outside or enjoy activities that came easily to her classmates. Natasha's condition had limited nearly every aspect of her life, including what she could eat and how active she could be.

"I didn't feel good," Natasha said. "I couldn't run. I couldn't swim. I couldn't eat chocolate."

Even so, she was a happy child.

"Honestly she was just trying to be a normal kid," said Chris Burleton, Natasha's grandmother, with whom Natasha lives in Oakfield to be closer to the specialists who treat her. "Our only hope was to get a new kidney."

In the principal's office that day, Chris and Jodi greeted Natasha. By then, Chris knew Jodi's kidney was a match for her. She handed Natasha a note from Jodi she'd read just moments before her granddaughter arrived in the room.

"It read, 'We are a match,'" Natasha said. "I'm like, 'Oh, my God.' I thought it was awesome, because a teacher in my school was giving me her kidney."

The news lifted a weight off Natasha's shoulders and answered her entire family's prayers. "It was relief. It was joy. It was happiness," Chris said.

But the process actually started months earlier, when

Jodi was driving home after work one evening and had an epiphany.

Sudden Decision

Jodi knew Natasha left school three times a week for dialysis. Each session was two hours long, and she couldn't survive without them. She had reached end-stage renal failure and needed a kidney donor. Jodi had been following Natasha's situation through coworkers. But it was through social media that she learned that Natasha's blood type was the same as hers, which meant her kidney was more likely to be a match.

She was thinking about that during the December drive home.

I need to try to help this girl, she thought.

Jodi's decision was sudden, unexpected—and absolute. "I pulled into the church parking lot, and I called my husband and said, 'I think I'm going to donate a kidney.' There was just something very strong about the pull. I had to do it."

In February, after she talked with her family and school administrators, Jodi underwent a series of tests at a local hospital to confirm her kidney was a perfect match for Natasha.

"I kept it all very secret," Jodi said. "I told my principal to make sure I could take time off for the transplant and my family."

She didn't want anyone to know her intentions—didn't want to get their hopes up—until she knew for sure she was a match for Natasha.

Then she waited.

The good news left Jodi in awe. "I could save her life," she said. "It was incredible."

A month before the transplant, Jodi's husband Rich organized a fundraiser to help with Natasha's medical costs. Many people in Oakfield turned out to support her and raised approximately $25,000.

A "Kidney Twin"

The transplant procedure took about six hours, and it went off without a hitch. "The doctor said the kidney started working right away," Chris said. "They were just amazed how well Natasha did after surgery."

Both Jodi and Natasha were released from the hospital in less than two weeks, and they've been close ever since. Natasha spends time with Jodi and her family, and she dreams about following in her footsteps someday.

"Mrs. Schmidt's a teacher," Natasha said. "I think I can be just like her and be a third-grade teacher. Maybe when I'm a teacher, I'll see her every day at school as grownups."

The donated kidney is expected to function safely for another fifteen to twenty years. Another transplant could be necessary after that, but for now Natasha is getting stronger every day. She's gaining weight and enjoying her new freedom from dialysis.

Jodi said she wants the best for Natasha, and it meant a great deal to help her. "I absolutely feel very connected to her. I really felt it was my path."

The kidney has offered Natasha a new lease on life, and she's healthy for the first time in years. "I was...happy when I got my new kidney," she said. "I never knew I could go swimming, but I did after I got it. Sometimes I can do flips and cartwheels, things I couldn't do before."

She's looking forward to joining the Girl Scouts, and she dances to music every chance she gets. She also has something very dear in Jodi, she said—a "kidney twin."

"Mrs. Schmidt's part of my family," Natasha said. "We'll always be connected like that."

❦

"You have not lived today until you've done something for someone who cannot repay you." –John Bunyan

Teen Gives up Marching Band Spot to Guide Blind Freshman

"Even though there are all
these bad things happening in
the world right now...there's
always going to be good..."

WHEN FOURTEEN-YEAR-OLD AUTUMN Michels is on the football field, in lockstep with the rest of Laingsburg High School's marching band, she can't see anything.

The band marches with quick steps, instruments in hand.

Autumn, blind since age four, moves with them in the clarinet section. Although the world is dark to her, there's plenty she hears and feels.

"There's this part where we're marching really, really

fast, and it feels like we're trampling over each other, sort of," she said. "I like to picture things as we're marching to the music. I like to imagine horses running through fields."

Seventeen-year-old Rachael Steffens knows exactly which section of the band's routine Autumn is describing. Sitting in Autumn's living room a few days before the band would perform its homecoming halftime show, she nodded. "That's the fast part we have trouble with," she said.

It's Rachael's senior year of marching band, her last before graduation, and she's on the field during routines too—but she's the only member of the school's 114-person band without an instrument.

Rachael's role is crucial, though, and to Autumn it's everything.

That's because she gave up performing in order to be Autumn's guide. On the field, Rachael stands right behind her with her hands on Autumn's shoulders, and gently steers her friend during performances.

Autumn's parents, Jason and Angie Michels, said Rachael is sacrificing memories she would have made playing percussion to help another student.

Rachael, however, said she won't remember any of what she gave up. What she will remember is her friendship with Autumn. "And I don't think it would have been as strong had we not been doing this, marching together," she added.

"She Doesn't Let Not Having Sight Bring Her Down"

On a Friday night in September, Autumn and Rachael sat together, legs crossed in the grass on the sidelines of their rural high school's football field, before the start of the homecoming game.

The weather was uncharacteristically warm, the temperature eighty degrees at 7:00 p.m., so band members received permission to wear red T-shirts and shorts instead of their standard heavy uniforms, complete with feathered caps.

"Can you imagine wearing our gear tonight?" Autumn asked Rachael, her brown hair pinned back, away from her face.

Rachael laughed. At ease with each other, they swayed to the beat of the music playing over the loudspeaker before the game.

Autumn and Rachael didn't know each other at all before summer band camp. That's when their band director asked Rachael if she would serve as Autumn's temporary guide on the field, just for the duration of camp.

Autumn was a freshman, and it was her first season of marching band. She loved music and had been playing the clarinet since sixth grade.

At home, her favorite spot is a swing in her backyard. She'll sit there for hours, she said, singing country songs while she sways back and forth in the wind.

Diagnosed at seven months with an inoperable optic nerve glioma, a slow-growing brain tumor around the optic nerve, Autumn never had very good vision. When she was four, she lost her sight completely. Doctors removed her optic nerves, along with some of the tumor, which slowed its progression.

Autumn's parents said her blindness hasn't stopped her from excelling and bringing light to everything and everyone she touches. According to them, she's the definition of an optimist. "She loves to motivate other people. She wants to inspire other people," Angie said.

"To keep other people happy makes me happy," Autumn added. "Beauty to me is happy."

When the two girls met, Autumn's sharp sense of humor stood out to Rachael. "She doesn't let not having sight bring her down," she said. "She likes to show people that she can make the jokes just as well as they can."

The two girls worked well together on the field, with Autumn teaching Rachael what she needed to do to help her while she marched.

A lot of marching is muscle memory, Autumn said, but she can't do it all.

"She knows where to go and which direction we're going," Rachael said. "She just doesn't necessarily know when to stop. She can't make sure there are no other people around her."

"I don't want to run into people," Autumn said. "That's a big one."

By the end of band camp, when Rachael firmly squeezed Autumn's shoulders, Autumn understood—thanks to hours of practice together—whether Rachael needed her to stop, turn, slow down, or speed up.

Autumn trusted her, and although she'd had other guides for marching drills or parades, they'd never been consistent or made her feel as comfortable during a routine as Rachael did.

Their friendship happened naturally, they said. "I feel like our personalities are a lot the same," Autumn said, "which helps quite a bit."

"And we're both funny and comfortable making jokes," Rachael added.

"You Can Find a Way to Do Anything"

Rachael said her decision to give up performing during her last season of marching band wasn't difficult to make. She's still on the field, still marching, and she gets to help her friend. "I like marching with Autumn a lot more," she said. Rachael enjoys swapping jokes with Autumn on the field during practice, and she loves watching her march.

Autumn feels the same way about Rachael. "Just getting to know her has been fun," she said.

Angie said it's the best situation for their daughter, who's experiencing marching band with a true friend by her side.

The genuine kindness behind Rachael's gesture and her friendship with Autumn is what makes people smile when they see the pair marching together, she said. "It's a lot for a teenage kid to want to help her. It takes initiative. This was never something we thought would happen."

Amy Brown, Rachael's mother, wasn't surprised. "People who know them are going to understand," she said. "This is their life every day. It's not just a one-time thing for these girls. This is who they are. Why can't everybody else be like that?"

Rachael thinks everyone can make a difference in someone else's life. "Even though there are all these bad things happening in the world right now…there's always going to be good to look to," she said. "You can find a way to do anything and make it work."

"Not all of us can do great things. But we can do small things with great love." –Mother Teresa

---

Veterinarian Goes Above and Beyond to Save a Pit Bull

IN THE VIDEO, Dr. Andy Mathis sits calmly, legs crossed, inside a large wire dog cage. He's dressed in jeans and a button-down shirt, with a thermos of coffee on the floor, as he eats cereal and milk out of a metal dog bowl in his hands.

The Georgia veterinarian is a peculiar sight for sure.

But it's the timid, anxious cellmate next to him who tugs your heartstrings during the six-minute encounter.

The little gray pit bull in the corner of the cage clearly doesn't want to be this close to Andy. She sits rigidly in the corner, her emaciated frame leaning into its safety. Her head is down, her eyes fixed on Andy as he picks up a spoon and eats.

He reaches over and casually places a bowl filled with dog food in front of her, then continues to eat. The pit bull's downcast eyes glance from the food to Andy and back again.

He casually scoops a handful of the food from the bowl onto the floor and offers it to her. Reluctantly she takes it.

Less than a minute passes before she eats from the bowl in earnest.

The rest of their meal is shared quietly, with Andy reaching over occasionally to gently run his hand over her back.

The video, uploaded to Granite Hills Animal Care's Facebook page, had no captioning and little explanation, but the moment it captured—a vet encouraging a frightened dog to trust sharing a meal with him—received a massive, unexpected response.

It was viewed a million times that first day, and in the weeks that followed, the pit bull, affectionately named Graycie Claire, became a viral sensation.

Major networks, including ABC, NBC, and CNN picked up the story. National newspapers and websites ran it too. Andy, praised for a simple, singular act of kindness, admitted he still wasn't sure why it garnered so much attention.

When you ask the small-town vet in northeast Georgia why he ate a meal with a sickly stray dog, he'll give you a simple, logical answer. "It was me socializing her," he said. "She'd been eating the whole week. Eating wasn't the problem. She always ate whatever I put in front of her, but not in front of people."

Learning to trust again, that's what Andy helped Graycie Claire do.

But he saved her life first.

Lifesaving Decision

Late one Friday, Andy received a phone call from a desperate woman. The dog she'd found lying on the side of a rural road outside of town was in bad shape. The animal's bones were visible beneath her soft gray coat. She was curled up in a ball, listless, and wouldn't move.

"She was able to throw a blanket over her and scoop her up," Andy said.

But the local animal shelter already had closed for the day.

"I said, 'You need to bring her in and let me have a look at her.'"

It wasn't the first time Andy, who's owned Granite Hills Animal Care for more than two decades, had taken in a stray and cared for it until he could adopt it out. There had been the occasional litter of kittens found on a doorstep or a lonely dog tied to a tree, he said.

But when Graycie Claire came through the doors of his

clinic, her temperature was low, and she was anemic and starving. Andy thought she might need a blood transfusion.

He had to make a decision quickly: put her to sleep or rush her to the local university's teaching vet hospital for reinforcements.

When he caught Graycie Claire's gaze, he saw the will to live. "She didn't have that sort of 'I give up' look in her eyes," he said. "I thought it was worth taking a chance."

So he took her to the hospital.

By the next day, Graycie Claire was eating on her own. By Sunday, she was stable and back at his clinic.

Andy's friends had named her during her hospital stay. "And being in the South, she needed a good Southern, two-part name," Andy said.

Graycie Claire's backstory is a mystery. She was wearing a purple collar and was clearly someone's pet before she was found. Did she run away from them? Was she abused? Neglected? There's no way to know for sure, but Graycie Claire was frightened of people. That was obvious.

When people were outside her cage, she sat in the corner, head down, eyes warily tracking unwanted visitors as they milled through the room. But when they left her, she'd bark at the other animals and move about her cage.

"When we opened up the cage, she'd back up like she was trying to get away from you," Andy said.

His shared meal with her was his first attempt at showing her people wouldn't hurt her.

"Dogs in animal shelters, sometimes they're just so traumatized, so broken, that it just takes them time to adjust," he explained.

Better Every Day

After the video of Andy's breakfast with Graycie Claire made the Internet rounds, he received countless phone calls. Well-meaning dog lovers from across the country wanted to adopt the pit bull.

"They would say, 'Oh, I love Graycie. We want to adopt her.'"

But Graycie wasn't ready for that then and still isn't now.

Three months after her rescue, she'd gained twenty pounds; she was still small but much healthier. She still prefers the company of other dogs to humans and has lingering health issues. She struggles with potty training but allows staff at the clinic to walk her three or four times a day.

New videos on the clinic's Facebook page are proof of her progress. They show a revived Graycie Claire, tail wagging and eyes bright, as she plays with other dogs. Her hesitation and fear are gone.

But Andy believes she needs the right family and plenty of other dogs to play with. "I think she'll end up liking people, but that will be through other dogs. They'll help her come along. Right now she's not in a big hurry to go anywhere."

Graycie Claire might never be ready to leave his care. And Andy is fine with that.

"If we can't adopt her out, I still might end up keeping her because she likes other dogs and being around here."

It's clear hers was a life worth saving. "She's getting better every day," Andy said.

What he did—saving Graycie Claire and nursing her back to health—was something he believes any good vet would have done. Compassion, he said, is part of the job.

"People said, 'Oh, we need more vets like you.' I was sort of shaking my head and thinking, *I'm like every other vet you know. You just don't see it and here you did.*"

"How far that little candle throws his beams! So shines a good deed in a weary world." –William Shakespeare

For a Pediatrician and a Paramedic, Kindness Comes Full Circle

A DEVOTED PEDIATRICIAN spends the night in a hospital, watching over a premature baby boy, just seven weeks old, who struggles to recover from a sudden high fever.

Thirty-six years later, a paramedic arrives at the scene of a car accident to help rescue a man pinned in his burning car after it collided with a semitruck.

The story of the pediatrician and the paramedic is a snapshot of kindness coming full circle. It is the unlikeliest of tales, a testament to what can happen when one person helps save another's life, only to have their life saved by that same person years later.

Dr. Michael Shannon and Chris Trokey's friendship is heartwarming. Proof that kind acts can lead to meaningful, lifelong connections.

"You Just Never Know"

"You just never know when things will come back around," Chris said.

The thirty-six-year-old knows what he's talking about. Today he's a paramedic with the Orange County Fire Authority in California, but he was born premature, weighing just three pounds, two ounces. He spent several weeks in the hospital before going home, only to be brought back at seven weeks with a dangerously high fever.

Michael remembers when Chris was admitted to the hospital. He stayed by Chris's side throughout the night, treating his extremely high fever until it broke the next day.

He continued as his pediatrician until Chris was a teenager. Chris remembers Michael as the "friendly, relaxed" doctor who always wore cowboy boots at the office—a man his parents trusted completely—but by adulthood he'd all but forgotten the doctor.

But the early morning call his fire department unit responded to years later isn't something he'll ever forget.

"A Really, Really Close Call"

Michael was driving to work at 5:30 a.m. when he turned a corner and a truck pulled out directly in front of him.

"The next thing I heard was the crash of glass and the sound of impact as I hit the truck," he said. "The dashboard of the car was sitting in my lap. But then I remember thinking, *I'm alive.*"

Michael's legs were on fire, and paramedics quickly approached the side of the car to break open the door. After they did, they removed him from the vehicle.

"I had trouble breathing, and I think I probably had some thoughts like, *Well, this is it.*"

The call came in late during Chris's shift; he'd been up all night. He and other members of his crew reached the scene of the accident within minutes. It was a bad one, said Chris, one of the first responders on the scene.

"We could see a bunch of people running around, screaming, 'He's on fire!'" he said.

The car's front end was smashed and crammed underneath a semitruck. The vehicle was on fire, and a man was pinned in the driver's seat, his legs trapped under crushed metal.

"It's not every day that you see a [situation] like that," Chris said. "You get there and you know it's different from most, more immediate. That's when you do what you do. It just comes. It was a really, really close call for Dr. Shannon. It was just perfect timing. I'm just really happy overall that it worked out. I'm so grateful we were able to get there when we did."

Chris helped remove Michael from the car, comforted

him while treating his wounds, and rode with him in the back of the ambulance on the way to the hospital, all the while monitoring his condition. He didn't realize it was his childhood doctor until they arrived at the ER.

"That's when I recognized his name," Chris said.

"Thank You for Everything"

A few days later, Chris visited Michael in the hospital, opening the conversation with a heartfelt thank-you to the doctor for his vigilance all those years ago when he was a sick infant.

"Thank you for everything you did for me and my parents when I was little," Chris told him. "You went above and beyond."

From his hospital bed, Michael admitted he was struck by the serendipity of the situation. "You just never think someone you're helping will come back and pass it forward to you," he said. "But the longer I've been doing this—the longer I've been doing this life—I see things happen every day that are not coincidence."

In the years since Chris helped save the doctor's life, Michael has visited him at the fire station once a year on the anniversary of the accident, delivering a thank-you meal to Chris and the entire station. It's a reminder, he said, that he'll always be thankful to them for saving his life.

It's changed both men, and even after Michael's full recovery, they've stayed in close touch. After Michael asked Chris to take part in a cancer research fundraiser for St. Baldrick's Foundation, the pair shaved their heads and raised several thousand dollars for the organization.

Chris still smiles when he thinks about their connection, what they did for each other. "It's a feel-good story for sure," he said. "Now he's my son's pediatrician." Kindness really comes full circle.

ॐ

"To this day, especially in times of disaster... I am always comforted by realizing that there are still so many helpers—so many caring people in this world." –Fred Rogers

UNIQUE WAYS OF SHOWING KINDNESS

Sticky Notes Become Beautiful Gesture of Kindness

CAN AN ORDINARY sticky note help feed the poor and homeless?

The staff at Rosa's Fresh Pizza on 11th Street in downtown Philadelphia think so.

The small eatery in one of the country's poorest cities has given away more than 75,000 pieces of pizza to people living on the city's streets. About a hundred homeless people eat at Rosa's every day.

The concept is simple. It's not expensive or complicated—and it works. A one-dollar donation at the counter prepays for a slice of pizza that will be offered to a homeless individual. The donor can write an encouraging message on a Post-it and stick it to the wall.

Owner Mason Wartman credits the kindness of one customer with the idea.

And today he sustains it.

The restaurant is proof, he says, that people want to help one another—they simply need a reminder of how easily it can be done.

Light-Bulb Moment

The walls inside Rosa's are covered with colorful Post-its, a sea of bright messages to the needy.

"God bless."

"We care."

"Pay it forward."

But when twenty-eight-year-old Mason stuck the very first one on the wall behind the front counter, it was out of necessity—a no-frills way of knowing just how many slices of pizza customers had donated.

Mason had left a three-year stint on Wall Street, where he had done "a lot of number crunching and document formatting for the analysts." His father owned a golf-course supply shop, and his grandfather owned a clothing store. "I wanted to own my own business but not right after college," he said.

But a pizza joint offering slices for a dollar each?

He knew there was a market in Philadelphia for the affordable, sensible idea. So he leased a 1,500-square-foot space and hired a handful of employees. The business, named after his mother, served everyone, with a number of homeless coming in each day to buy pizza.

One Sunday, a customer offered to prepay for a slice of pizza for someone in need.

"They saw that we served a lot of homeless people because it was a portable food," Mason said. "Sometimes [the homeless] came in short on change. He offered to prepay a slice for the next homeless person who came in."

It was a light-bulb moment. "I immediately thought the idea was very clever," Mason said. "I thought it could help people."

He took the idea and ran with it, placing a sign in the dining area explaining the "pay-it-forward" pizza option.

Customers could prepay for slices of pizza, which would go to customers without the means to pay for it.

To keep track of the prepaid slices, Post-its were handed to customers who wanted to take part. They'd pay an extra dollar and write a note on the slip of paper. The messages were placed behind the counter, then removed and given to homeless people who entered to buy pizza.

"It was well received, so I kept doing it," Mason said.

Food and Kindness

Within a month, five hundred Post-its had been affixed, creating a colorful collage of generosity. It was a visible reminder of the need that existed—and the fact that people wanted to help meet it. Most of the notes were covered in flour and crinkling around the edges with moisture from the ovens. "The kitchen walls were totally covered in Post-it notes," Mason said.

The homeless customers who were handed the message, along with a slice of pizza, were grateful—and touched. "They came to rely on us for food, and it's one less worry on their minds," Mason said.

Thirty-nine-year-old Eddie Dunn was one of those customers. Although he's been stable and off the streets for more than a year, he remembers the days when his only meal was the pizza he ate at Rosa's.

"I was homeless," he said. "I was downtown. I was panhandling with a sign, and I was an off-and-on heroin user. Obviously the money I was making wasn't going to food." Kindness can be hard to come by when you're homeless, he added. "You get a lot of dirty looks. But every once in a while, you come across people like Mason who treat you like a person."

Eddie has never forgotten the kindness of Mason and all the people who paid it forward. When he finally conquered his drug addiction, he came back to Rosa's, stood at the front counter, and paid for his own slice of pizza.

Then he pulled out another dollar and prepaid for one more, adding a Post-it to the wall.

"Paying it forward impacts people," he said. "People may not remember what you said or what you did, but they remember how you treat them."

Generosity Recognized

Rosa's generosity has brought the business notoriety. The restaurant has been featured in local newspapers, local blogs, and even on the national news.

The attention has been great for the business. "It blew up," Mason said. "It's been just crazy ever since."

The Post-its are symbolic these days. Although customers still write encouraging messages for the homeless on them, the prepaid slices are now kept track of in a computer.

The gesture is catching on elsewhere. "I've gotten emails from a bunch of different restaurants all around the country," Mason said. "They want to implement similar programs. I think it's inspired other people to try and replicate it, and I think it'll continue to."

Mason will do his part to perpetuate the kindness. He said the concept has helped him realize that small contributions—one dollar, one slice of pizza—can be significant to someone in need. He plans to open a second Rosa's on the west side of the city, offering the same "pay-it-forward" policy.

The young business owner wants to make the world a better place. "There's a lot that everyone has to offer society," he said. "No one should really be overlooked or ignored for any reason, especially if they're experiencing pain or hurt or anguish, and there's a lot that we can gain by helping them. That's when everyone benefits the most."

> "Sometimes a small thing you do can mean everything in another person's life." —Maya Angelou

Bikers Protect Abused Children

"There's no better feeling in my world."

THEY HAVE TATTOOS, are clad in leather, and the motorcycles they ride are loud, but if you expect them to apologize for their imposing appearance, think again.

That big, bad biker image?

"That image makes this work."

"Klimoman" is six foot five and weighs 335 pounds. His road name is the only one he'll share. On a Tuesday night in September, he sat in a coffee shop in Howell, Michigan, discussing the stereotypes that surround bikers.

"For the most part, bikers really don't care what you think," he said. "I think those that love to ride with a passion are drawn to it. I don't live my life worrying if that guy behind the counter thinks I'm all right."

But what if those preconceived notions could be put to good use? What if they could heal suffering?

Welcome to Bikers Against Child Abuse International (BACA).

The brother and sisterhood of bikers has one goal: to create a safe environment for children who've been abused. Founded in 1995 in Utah, the organization has chapters in the United States and seventeen other countries.

Klimoman, Gus, and Mayor, three mid-Michigan men who've been riding motorcycles for more than eight decades combined, helped start Wayne County's BACA chapter. It's the state's first, and they've assisted more than thirty-five children, ages five to eighteen.

You'll find them, bikes parked in front of a child's house, keeping watch while they sleep, or sitting in a courtroom wearing full biker attire while a child on the witness stand details the abuse he or she endured.

Forty-eight-year-old Klimoman recalled a story one BACA member told about being in a courtroom while an abused boy was about to testify. When the judge asked the youngster if he was afraid to testify in front of his abuser, he answered, "No. My friends are much scarier than him."

BACA members say this is proof that their tough biker image gives them an undeniable advantage when it comes to helping abused children.

Helping "Heroes"

Sixty-year-old Mayor has been riding motorcycles since age thirteen. He bought his first bike before he owned a car, and today he's the president of BACA's Wayne County chapter. Every one of the group's twenty-four members reached out to BACA's leadership to ask how they could get involved.

Their reasons vary, he said. His are intensely personal.

"A lot of people don't understand what it is to be afraid of your dad, what he's going to do to you," Mayor said. "I was one of those kids at one time."

He declined to go into details, but said he was ten years old when the abuse started. He left home by sixteen. "I haven't been back. I managed to finish school and went to college on my own. I did it all on my own. Now I want to be able to help these kids, you know?"

BACA addresses something Mayor knows all too well: the fear that abused children feel even after they've escaped the pull of their abusers.

The organization's members are as young as twenty and as old as seventy-five. In their daily lives, they maintain a range of careers, from management to blue-collar jobs. Some of them have children, and they all ride motorcycles.

Everyone in BACA must submit to state and federal background checks, and they undergo continual training regarding everything from courtroom etiquette to how they should interact with abused children.

The organization calls the kids they help "heroes," and BACA members see them that way too.

BACA connects with abused children in different ways. Sometimes they receive referrals from local police departments and child advocacy groups. They also take calls from families through a hotline, but every "hero" is connected to an active court case that involves some kind of abuse.

"We work in conjunction with everyone," Klimoman said. "The cops, the courts, the advocacy groups. We'll go anywhere for a hero. We're not going to turn anybody down."

And he means it.

It's not a seasonal gig. BACA members ride wherever and whenever a child needs them—in the cold, in the rain, in the middle of the night.

"We've rode in rain, snow, for hours," Klimoman said. "If the hero calls us and they're having fear, we're there. If we say we're going to be there, we show up at all costs."

That usually starts with an all-hands-on-deck visit with the child. Every member of the chapter takes part in the bike ride to meet the boy or girl.

"We raise hell," Klimoman said. "Make a lot of noise coming down the street."

Then BACA welcomes the child into the organization, giving them their own vest with a road name of their choosing sewn on a patch on the front.

"When we walk up, we don't fist-bump," Klimoman said. "We don't put our hand up to shake their hand. We let them make the first action, because they are the ones in charge. If they're hugging Mom and Dad's leg, and they don't want to talk to us, that's fine. If they want to be in the house, peeking through the window, looking at us? That's fine. We show up. That's what we do."

It's important to give the children that freedom, said Gus. "We're there to empower the child, and we let them make the choices on how the interaction goes and what they want to do."

"We give their ability to make their own decisions back to them," Mayor added. "The one thing that bothered me the most as a kid was the fear. I was always afraid. We can walk in there and make that fear go way."

A Steady Presence

In the courtroom, BACA's members are a support system. They escort children to court dates and parole hearings, providing a friendly face during what can be a terrifying experience. While testifying, younger children hold teddy bears BACA members have given them; teenagers wear pins they've received.

"They know, after everything's done, we'll be there regardless of whatever happens," Gus said. "We really aren't there for the process. We're there for the kid. They can do what they need to do; they can focus on us."

Their steady presence has made a difference.

"I want to thank you for all you have done for my step-daughter," reads a letter one parent wrote to the chapter. "Before your group entered her life, she did not sleep in her own bed. Her mom and I could go nowhere without her attached to our hips. Now that you have been a part of her life, she feels safer. She sleeps in her own bed and is doing some things on her own."

Klimoman says those are the stories that make BACA members proud. "We fill the gaps that police and child protective services can't. If a kid can't sleep at night because they're deathly afraid and you call the police, they're not going to come. You call us, we'll be there. We'll surround that house and watch it twenty-four hours a day."

Mayor said his involvement has been rewarding in ways he'd never imagined. "I'm sixty years old, but this organization, these friends that I call brothers and sisters, have helped me, and these kids have helped me heal."

Members of the Wayne County chapter said BACA will spread throughout Michigan. They're working to help start four more chapters in cities across the state.

It's reassuring, Klimoman said, and encouraging—the knowledge that BACA's reach is growing. "To me, it makes my heart feel great to see these children make a turnaround and be kids again," he said. "That's an awesome feeling. There's no better feeling in my world."

✦

"There is more good than bad in this world, more light than darkness, and you can make more light." –Peter H. Reynolds

A Labor of Love with Angel Gowns

"It lifts me to know that I'm touching somebody in a big way,"

KATHY CHAREST WEPT while creating her first angel gown.

She sat at her sewing machine, cutting up a 1950s wedding dress and binding small pieces of satin together, then adding delicate details: a little lace, a stitched design, some ribbon. Tears seeped out of the corners of her eyes and flowed down her cheeks while she worked, slowly but carefully, intent on perfection.

When she finished, the tiny cream-colored gown she'd made was neatly tucked into a box, then delivered to a mother who was mourning the loss of her newborn.

Kathy, founder of Angel Gowns Ministry to Brevard

County, Florida, has been making delicate burial outfits for infant boys and girls since 2014. Although she's never met the families who've received them, the enormity of their loss is with her every time she and a core group of volunteers make one.

"I believe that every little bit of life is to be cherished," Kathy said. "This is the first and last thing someone is ever going to put on your child. I want each gown to be simply beautiful."

And because most of the material for Kathy's creations comes from donated wedding dresses, there's a great deal of beauty to work with.

The satin, silk, pearls, and lace that make up the dresses become part of each angel outfit and bonnet gifted to grieving families in Brevard County and around the country; they go wherever the need is.

Kathy admits the idea to turn wedding dresses into delicate burial gowns for infants isn't hers. It belongs to a nurse in Washington state, Michelle Matthews, who used her own wedding dress to begin sewing angel burial outfits for babies who had died during pregnancy or shortly after birth at the hospital where she worked.

Kathy had been sewing for decades when she read about Michelle's efforts, then decided to follow suit. "You can only make so many things for your family and friends," she said, "and I wanted to bless somebody."

A Powerful Image

"Can you imagine?" Kathy said. "I can't imagine giving birth and holding that teeny, tiny baby and having to say goodbye."

The heartbreaking reality of losing a newborn compelled Kathy, a mom herself, to start Angel Gowns.

She contacted Michelle, who sent her a few sewing patterns for the outfits. She then collected several wedding dresses from friends and family and began to sew.

For two years, Kathy worked steadily—and solo—donating her unique gowns to local organizations and hospitals already in contact with families grieving the loss of a newborn.

It was hard at first, she admitted. The work was emotional, and it felt personal. Many of the gowns are created for infants weighing just a few ounces. Having experienced a miscarriage herself, Kathy related to the parents who would receive them and understood the magnitude of their loss firsthand.

"I do understand what it is to have a loss," she said. "No matter how early it is, that's your child, that's your little baby."

One day a local reporter who had heard about Angel Gowns visited Kathy and wrote about the impact she was making.

"Would you welcome some help?" asked the reporter.

"Absolutely," Kathy said.

Seventy-six-year-old Amparo Eisenmann was one of a few dozen area women who reached out to Kathy after the article was published. Getting involved and creating angel gowns lifted her out of a depression she'd struggled with after a hip replacement made being active difficult.

"I can't do what I used to do," Amparo said. "I was very active, walking. When I read the story about Kathy, I thought, *I can do it from home.* It takes me a while, but I like to sew."

Kathy said Amparo is a true seamstress, and her work is exquisite.

Amparo added that the volunteer work has been a blessing. "When I feel sad, I come to my sewing room," she said. "It's been the best thing. I try to make the dresses as beautiful as they can be so the parents feel really, really good that their baby is in it."

Joan Baron, sixty-four, is another of Kathy's helpers. Retired from her job in city government and a mother of two, she said the grieving families "touched her heart" and she needed to get involved.

"All I needed was a pattern and I was off," she said. "It's unbelievable what the parents go through. I kind of get worked up about it, but I think of the goodness I'm doing and feel privileged to be a part of this group."

Making a Difference

At least once a month, the women meet at Kathy's house in Melbourne, Florida. They pass around finished gowns and praise them, create new patterns to work from, and sew together.

"We are a mix of vastly different personalities," Kathy said. "But I know their hearts. I cry a lot with these ladies. There's so much hugging and tears. There's so much depth in their lives, and I love that they share it with me. I love that this effort has come to my little corner of the world."

Although sewing the outfits can be somber work, Kathy also appreciates the joy she feels in doing it. "It lifts me to know that I'm touching somebody in a big way," she said. "To me, this is just so beautiful, and it feels so important for me to create these gowns and take special care with them."

Kathy said her group doesn't rush a single outfit, taking time with every stitch and detail.

Every once in a while, they get a thank-you—a card or handwritten note from a grieving but forever grateful parent who dressed their infant in an angel gown before saying goodbye.

"Kathy," one reads. "You don't know me and I don't know you, but our lives are forever entwined through my precious baby girl. Dressing her in your gown left us with so much peace."

"When I get these things, I share them with the sewing group because I want them to know we really are making a difference," Kathy said. "Our goal is to make each gown perfect for these families. That brings me joy."

"So the darkness shall be the light, and the stillness the dancing." –T. S. Eliot

Dad Finds a Brilliant Way to Use Leftover Crayons to Help Others

THE TRIANGULAR CRAYONS were thick and easy to grasp.

The six-year-old boy at the table had been suffering with chronic illness, in and out of hospitals since birth. The day before his next surgery, Kellye Carroll sat with him. She watched as he used the bright crayons to draw a map of UCLA Mattel Children's Hospital.

"He would take me through the maps," she said. "They were very intricate, but it was calming for him. He was actually drawing something therapeutic; a map that shows how he'll get back to his playroom; his safe place, once he's better."

This is the story Kellye, the hospital's director of child life programs, told to illustrate the impact, and the value, of The Crayon Initiative.

It's a nonprofit that's provided thousands of new

crayons to children's hospitals around the United States. The organization is the brainchild of Bryan Ware, a businessman and father of two, who took a simple idea and ran with it.

A Question and a Thought

Why crayons?

Bryan was celebrating his fortieth birthday at a restaurant where crayons sat on the table, awaiting the next youngster dining there.

That evening he pondered their fate. *What happens to these crayons at the end of the night?*

The answer? After one use, every single crayon ended up in the trash.

Bryan saw nothing but wasted potential. How many art classrooms could benefit from those castaways? He wanted to find a way to put those crayons to good use while also promoting the power of art with young people. It was something Bryan and his wife, Marissa, had long believed was important but undervalued.

He left the restaurant with a handful of crayons in his pocket. For a year, they sat on his desk at his packaging and product-design consulting firm.

And then he successfully found a way to make a difference with them.

He created The Crayon Initiative, a nonprofit that recycles restaurant crayons from across the country and supplies thousands of boxes of new crayons to children's hospitals.

The unique movement puts smiles on thousands of children's faces and has drawn praise from around the world. It's also received a slew of national media attention that has surprised and puzzled Bryan. "But then you gotta step back and say, 'It's cool and it's working and it's impacting people. Just roll with it.'"

Bringing Color into Hospitals

Bryan started out wanting to give back to schools in need of art supplies. That was before a good friend, a child specialist at an area hospital, pointed out that the child life departments in most hospitals have limited budgets. They stretch those dollars to provide necessities for families, comfort to sick children, and games for the countless hours young patients spend there waiting for—or undergoing—treatment.

"I started asking around and guess what? All hospitals operate this way," Bryan said.

Crayons are a valuable commodity in children's hospitals. Just ask Kellye. "Do you know how many crayons we go through or what kind of tool that is for child life programs?" she asked. "The benefit of having crayons in any part of the hospital can't be overstated. Everyone knows what to do with a crayon. You don't have to speak the same language. A crayon is one of the first things we go to."

Still, Kellye didn't take Bryan seriously when he approached her with his idea. *There's no way he'll be able to make enough of them*, she thought.

Bryan, however, was determined to follow through on his promise. He reached out to BJ's Restaurants and Brewhouse with a simple request: "Stop throwing your used crayons away every day. Give them to me instead."

The company readily agreed.

Bryan consulted with lawyers about working toward the creation of a nonprofit. They loved the idea but wondered why he didn't want to make any money off the endeavor.

"No, no, no," he said. "We're going to give it all away."

The Devil is in the details—and they were what mattered next. It took the better part of a year for Bryan to figure them out. How would he melt so many crayons? How would he remove all the paper wrappers? How would he create the right mold for reshaping them?

There was plenty of trial and error, stopping and starting.

The work takes place in Bryan's own kitchen, after the entire room is draped to contain the mess. Colorful pots of melted wax—red, green, yellow, blue—sit in saucepans on the stovetop.

The molds are special, thicker and longer than your standard crayon and triangular to make sure little fingers can easily grasp and color with them. The new boxes, which hold eight crayons each, are packed and shipped from the family's living room in San Francisco.

The first time Kellye visited Bryan's kitchen, sitting through a crayon-making session, she became a believer.

"It almost brought tears to my eyes," she said. "I thought, *Oh, my gosh! This is amazing.*"

UCLA Mattel Children's Hospital received its first shipment of dozens of crayons a few months later.

A Movement

Bryan will tell you he's an engineer—a practical, hands-on person. He saw a problem and found a solution. At its core, that's how The Crayon Initiative was born.

But Bryan said its value is best measured by the smiles of patients when they pull a crayon out of a box and begin coloring or drawing. "It definitely drives home the work we're doing."

The Crayon Initiative recently supplied more than

6,000 boxes of new crayons—that's more than 60,000 crayons—to thirty hospitals around the country. Bryan said it's only a matter of time before the organization donates to hundreds of hospitals.

People across the country are getting involved as well. Restaurants from coast to coast donate used crayons to Bryan, and random people send them to him in envelopes.

Sorting "parties" are held regularly in San Francisco. Dozens of people take part, helping to further the initiative. Bryan is looking for larger headquarters for the nonprofit, where melting, pouring, sorting, and shipping can take place.

"We talk about The Crayon Initiative kind of as a movement," he said. "I see a shift happening. I have people calling from South Africa and Europe and Asia, saying, 'We want to do this. How do we get started?'"

It's been "heartwarming," he said, to the see the faces of children in the hospital when they take hold of a crayon and get lost in art and creation. "It's so good to see. It gives them an escape from their daily life that they need there."

Kellye, who eventually joined the nonprofit's board of directors, isn't surprised. Bryan simply "gets it." "I believe in what he's doing," she said.

Bryan says the initiative has made an incredible difference in the lives of brave children across the country and he's surprised by the bonds he's formed with many of them. "I've met these kids, built a relationship with them. That part was not something I expected."

❧

"Children are the flowers of life! They bring joy and happiness to our world. Let's be kind to them. Let's make them happy, and let's help them to save that child inside for the rest of their lives!" –Unknown

---

College Student Mows Lawns Free of Charge

"I don't know how to say it, but it just makes me feel good to give back."

IF YOU ASK twenty-six-year-old Rodney Smith Jr. why he started cutting lawns for the elderly, people with disabilities, and single mothers free of charge, he'll give you a brief, direct answer: "I'm just doing what I have to do to give back."

But when you ask him what inspired the idea, he'll paint a vivid picture of need that puts his endeavor, Raising Men Lawn Care Service, into clear perspective.

One summer, when Rodney was working toward his bachelor's degree in computer science at Alabama A&M, he noticed an older neighbor having trouble mowing his lawn in their Huntsville neighborhood. "He was taking his time, doing it really slow, and it was obvious he was really struggling," he said.

It bothered Rodney, a native of Bermuda. Back home, goodwill is a way of life; people help one another. "It's just the way in Bermuda," he said.

Someone should help this man and people like him, he thought.

Rodney decided it might as well be him, so he posted a message on social media: "If anyone knows somebody who's elderly or a single mother, let me know, and I'll cut their lawn for free."

He set a goal. Between classes, he'd work toward cutting forty lawns for people who needed help.

Through Facebook, he received messages with addresses and worked through them when he could. He didn't have his own lawnmower, so he used the equipment people had when he knocked on their doors.

"I'd get out of class and go cut grass and then go to my next class," Rodney said. "I'd cut grass all weekend long."

It was time consuming but worthwhile. Many of the people Rodney helped told him they were on fixed incomes. They struggled to pay monthly living expenses and couldn't afford to pay for lawn care, but they also couldn't afford the fines they'd face if their lawns weren't maintained. Many of them couldn't physically do it themselves.

Rodney's offers were unexpected but welcomed.

Eventually he found a secondhand lawn mower for sale, and when the seller learned why Rodney wanted it, he gave it to him for free.

A month later, he'd mowed nearly two dozen lawns—and an idea began to take shape.

Raising Men

Over time, Rodney's one-man effort became Raising Men Lawn Care Service.

The idea was simple: male children and teenagers, ages seven to seventeen, could join the group and offer free lawn care to people who struggled to do the work themselves. In turn, they gained character, compassion, and mentorship from older volunteers involved in the effort.

"Some of the young men we work with, they don't have a positive male figure in their lives," Rodney said. "It's having a positive impact on them. When an elderly person says, 'Thank you for what you've done,' their faces light right up.' We see them gain maturity."

Raising Men Lawn Care Service's Facebook page is filled with examples of that. Photographs of youngsters who cut lawns through the program and their stories fill its feed.

For several months, the program operated under the radar.

Then that changed.

On social media, Rodney shared a photo of an elderly woman his group had assisted, with a caption explaining the effort. It was shared by thousands and, within two days, by a million people. "We literally just went viral overnight," Rodney said.

He was shocked when national media outlets reached out to him and publicized his effort. "All we're doing is cutting grass and helping people out," he said.

But its brilliant simplicity might be why Raising Men Lawn Care Service has garnered so much attention.

Rodney said people don't give back as much as they should. "A lot of people say it gives hope, that there's still good out there in the world. I think it's important because someday we're going to be that person who needs the help. Hopefully, when we're there, somebody's willing to help us."

A Movement

In the months since his effort gained global exposure, Rodney has raised more than $50,000 through an online fundraising campaign.

The money will help support his dream of turning the lawn care service into an official nonprofit with multiple chapters around the country. To date, there are at least four—in Alabama, Florida, Michigan, and Bermuda.

"There are elderly people all over the world who need help," Rodney said. "That's the goal, to expand everywhere."

The Alabama chapter includes more than twenty-five young men from various backgrounds, some from poor neighborhoods and others from middle-class areas. Some are still in elementary school, others nearly eighteen. They use a riding lawn mower and smaller mowers, and a truck to transport the equipment—all donated.

Rodney often takes the time to talk with the people his group helps. Each one has a unique story and unique challenges, and recipients often struggle financially. "We have heard a lot of people say, 'It's hard right now,'" he said.

That's reason enough, he said, to help them.

"I think a lot of people, if they're going to give, they expect to receive," Rodney said. "We don't expect to receive. I don't know how to say it, but it just makes me feel good to give back."

Rodney plans to return to school to pursue a master's degree in social work. Once Raising Men Lawn Care Services becomes a nonprofit, he'll stay at the helm and lead it forward.

The sky's the limit, he said. "I would never have thought it would be this big, but it's good because it inspires people to get out and make a difference. I'm doing something small that's changing the world. It makes me feel good because we're starting a movement."

"One of the secrets of life is that all that is really worth doing is what we do for others." –Lewis Carroll

KINDNESS
MOVEMENTS

Friends Surprise Strangers by Paying for Their Groceries

"I can't tell you how fulfilling it was. We knew we were doing the right thing."

NERVOUS BUT READY, he stands in line behind a stranger in the supermarket checkout aisle.

Thirty-five-year-old Disty Simpson waits as the cashier finishes ringing up the person's order, and then, with a smile, he speaks up. "Hold on," he says, leaning in with some cash as the customer starts to swipe her card through the machine as payment. "That's broken. You don't want to use that. I'm taking care of you today."

More often than not, the recipient of Disty's goodwill looks at him speechless and confused as the gesture sinks in.

Disty, wearing jeans and a T-shirt, his black hair styled in a tall Mohawk, often walks away smiling, delivering a "God bless you" before he exits.

In his wake, there are tears, huge smiles, and amazement.

Then he gets in line again, behind another unsuspecting shopper.

"After that, it's like you're a kid who jumps in line again after the ride is over," Disty said. "You're not scared anymore and you can't wait to do it again."

Kindness feels good, he said.

It also can be infectious, and that's what Disty and two of his friends, Matt Danuser and Felix Cornejo, were counting on when Fill My Basket started. The grassroots, donation-driven movement, through which the three men pay people's grocery bills, sends a clear message: not only do good deeds matter, but they also can be contagious.

"I'm Going to Do This"

Disty still thinks about a man who was captured on camera paying for a random person's groceries and the video of him he watched online. He and Matt saw the same viral video; it was making the rounds on social media, and watching it changed them both.

"It stole my heart," Disty said. "I was emotional. I was crying."

It was the topic of conversation a few days later when Matt ran into Disty. The two men went to the same Oklahoma high school together but hadn't seen each other in a while.

"I swear I'm going to do this," Matt told him.

Disty volunteered to help.

A month later, Matt called his former classmate and set a date for their act of grocery-store goodwill. He'd recently received a bonus check at work; it was just enough, he told Disty, to make a difference.

Disty pitched in some of his own money and called Felix, another former classmate, and asked him to come along.

Felix said once he heard what they were planning to do he readily agreed. "I liked what he was coming at me with," he said. He also understood how difficult it can be to afford groceries. Two years earlier, Felix had gone through a period of financially instability. He got through it, but remembered the struggle.

"I know what it's like to go to the store with ten dollars and literally that's all you have," he said. "When we did this, I knew we would touch people."

During that first trip to an Oklahoma City grocery store, the three friends picked up the tab for a couple with several small children and another on the way.

"The experience was amazing," Disty said. "I can't tell you how fulfilling it was. We knew we were doing the right thing."

The trio left, committing to do it again.

Their random act caught the attention of the staff at a local TV station, and within a few days, reporters were talking about it on the air. Viewers were taken with the story and donated money to their cause. In the months that followed that rush of support, Fill My Basket began to take shape, and the movement has functioned solely on donations ever since.

With every visit to a grocery store, Disty and Matt are able to help fifteen to twenty people they've singled out, including families with kids, and individuals with just a few items, always surprising them just as they're about to pay their bill. Sometimes the recipient has only a gallon of milk in his or her cart, while others have a conveyor belt filled with items that cost as much as $350.

Disty and Matt stay in touch with some of the people they've helped, and some of them have donated to Fill My Basket. Hearing what their efforts have meant to families has inspired them to keep paying it forward.

"When you do something kind, there's a reward," Disty said. "We believe what you give you get back. It's these little stories and the feedback of people we've helped that make it worthwhile. For us, it's the message. We're trying to deliver a message, and if the message is strong, it has to be infectious."

Paying It Forward

These days, Fill My Basket encounters often are captured on video. A cameraman tags along, keeping his distance while filming, and trains the lens on the people Disty and Matt stand behind at the cash register. The videos show the customers' shock, tears, joy, and thank-yous.

Some of those exchanges have been featured in a video the group has used to promote what they hope will start a movement of kindness. Disty and Matt want to inspire viewers to do something for someone else.

"We want other people to see it," Disty said. "I think it's about the act itself. There's a message there of love, of paying it forward, of random acts."

It's a message the three men hope to impart to their children, family, friends, and strangers.

Fill My Basket is just one example of how anyone can make a difference, Felix said, and his children—seven and nine years old—are paying attention.

"They love it," he said. "It's been a blessing being a part of this."

Disty hopes Fill My Basket is a wake-up call for many

people who've been so swept up living busy, modern lives that they might have forgotten humanity's first obligation: to take care of one another.

"We don't want people to lose sight of that," he said. "Everything's moving at the speed of light. Everyone is walking around with their faces in their phones, not really paying attention to each other. We want people to see each other."

"Your acts of kindness are iridescent wings of divine love, which linger and continue to uplift others long after your sharing." –Rumi

A Compassionate Path to Reducing Homelessness

Donald Roberts had been homeless, on and off, for years all over the country.

Medical issues and job losses plagued him. In Texas and Arizona, he lived on the streets, struggling to find food and a place to sleep. He was dirty and in a constant state of movement, looking for the next meal or shelter.

Then he came to Utah.

There he lives in a small apartment—his home—and that's everything to him. "I actually think it's a miracle," he said.

Lofty praise for a lofty goal the state set in motion more than a decade ago: to help the chronically homeless—people who have been without a home for a year or more.

"Why Can't We Do What People Are Asking?"

You simply have to dig into the heart of the matter, said Lloyd Pendleton.

For nine years, he worked as Utah's Homeless Task Force director and spent a year working one-on-one with the state's homeless at local shelters.

What did he learn?

"These are regular people who happen to be without a house right now," Lloyd said. "They have mental health issues, substance abuse issues, yes, but when you get to know them rather than driving by and calling them names, telling them to get a job, you see they're people. They still have feelings and like to be treated like individuals, human beings."

What they need is simple: housing.

That's what Utah has done. The state's chronically homeless are being given homes.

It's an effort Lloyd spearheaded—and these days people are paying attention, because, since 2005 the state's chronically homeless population, which includes individuals and families, has decreased by 91 percent. That's down from 1,932 chronically homeless individuals to just 178 in a recent count.

The model, called Housing First, was developed by Sam Tsemberis, a New York–based social researcher. He's worked with New York City's homeless, people with serious medical and addiction issues. When he asked them what they needed, their answer was almost always the same: "I need a place to live."

State and federal programs offered housing assistance, Sam said, but they required homeless individuals to get treatment first—for all their issues. Fix your addiction. Get medical treatment for your health issues. Then we'll help house you. That was how the system worked.

"I thought, *Why can't we do what people are asking?*" Sam said. "I listened to people and thought we should help them in the way they were asking for help, not the way we thought we should help them."

What if, he asked, the homeless received homes first—and then, when they were safe and secure, the government reached out to help them stabilize their lives?

He worked on the concept for ten years, a controlled effort involving fifty chronically homeless people the first year. By year three, it was clear that Housing First was working. Eighty-five percent of the people housed through the study were still stable, compared to just 40 percent of the homeless who were working their way through traditional housing-assistance programs.

"We found we were doing twice as well," Sam said. "We were blown away."

A Real Solution

By the time Lloyd met Sam, during a conference on homelessness, the approach appeared to be a real savings for society as well. Data showed that fewer chronically homeless people living on the streets would lead to a substantial decrease in emergency room visits, hospital stays, and arrests.

That saves money.

Lloyd saw a real solution. He went back to Utah and set about implementing a pilot program: putting seventeen chronically homeless individuals in small apartments for almost two years. The program cost $150,000, and at the end of those two years, all the people living in those apartments were stable, still housed, and in some cases, finally addressing the issues that had kept them on the streets.

The results didn't surprise Lloyd. For the chronically homeless, which makes up twenty percent of the homeless population nationwide, the instability of a life on the streets makes a real life impossible, he said. They can't address addiction or health issues until they're no longer homeless.

"Getting them into housing, where they feel safe—they don't get beaten up; they can shut that door and take a shower and be safe—then, when they realize those basic needs are already taken care of, they say, 'All right. Now I can start to deal with my addiction, my mental health.'"

Case managers met with these individuals on a weekly basis and developed relationships with them. "You build a community of support for them," Lloyd said.

Utah eventually expanded the program. They opened one hundred more housing units, and over the last decade the effort has expanded across the state.

The program has received tremendous support ever since. "We had committed to do it, and the pilot was started to teach us how to do it," said Lloyd, who worked on the effort for a decade.

Compassionate Success

Donald's home gives him something he's never had: security and a sense of self-worth. "It helps a person's self-esteem when they have their own place," he said. "When you give a person a home, they know they're safe. They have a place to sleep, a place to be. Now they can go out and find a job."

Lloyd said he's seen the truth in Donald's statement. People placed in housing have relearned how to interact with others again—those living in neighboring apartments through the program and the advocates with whom they meet, thanks to the housing effort.

Homeless advocates visit them often, bringing meals, a listening ear, and hugs. "One guy told me, after an advocate hugged him, 'That's the first human being I've touched in two years,'" Lloyd said. "It's so stunning. They've been so isolated."

The effort helps formerly homeless people feel they're a part of society again and supports them as they find their way there.

Cities around the country have successfully adopted the Housing First model. But Utah's success is unique, Sam said, because it represents a widespread effort throughout the state. "I think this is how change happens. The success of the program builds momentum, and that brings in more and more stakeholders."

Lloyd now serves as a consultant, speaking with civic groups and government leaders across the United States about how Housing First can be implemented. "I'm speaking all over the country," he said. "I share this story."

There's plenty of interest too. He fields several calls a day from representatives from various cities interested in adopting Housing First programs.

There's little question Utah's approach has changed lives.

Just ask Donald. "It's the only state I know of that actually helps the homeless by putting them in a home, and that's fantastic," he said. "They care."

A compassionate approach can work anywhere, as long as advocates are devoted to the effort, Lloyd said. For him it's a humanitarian issue. "When we have anybody hurting in the community, then we're all suffering," he said. "I see them as my brother and my sister... It's not my place to condemn and judge. It's mine to bring hope."

"Do all the good you can, by all the means you can, in all the ways you can, in all the places you can, at all the times you can, to all the people you can, as long as you ever can." –Unknown

Adams Acts

FOR MORE THAN two decades, Lara Capuano has held tightly to one of her most precious memories of older brother Adam.

In it, she's sitting atop his shoulders as they're walking home from her friend's house. They'd spent the day there, jumping on a backyard trampoline together.

"We were laughing so hard," Lara said. "The whole time. He and I had a really special relationship."

That's how she remembers Adam: good-natured, caring, thoughtful.

But it was Adam Provencal's untimely death on Halloween night in 1992, when he was just seventeen, that made national headlines.

He was shot and killed by a stranger in Grand Haven, Michigan, when he knocked on the man's front door to apologize after his classmates had thrown toilet paper into a tree on the property.

Lara was just eleven when Adam died. Today she's a wife and a mother. She's also the creator of Adams Acts, a movement that has turned her family's tragedy into a rally cry for kindness—one that people around the world have supported.

Every October, for thirty-one days, Lara honors Adam's memory. Friends, family, and strangers do too. Their random acts of kindness keep her big brother's spirit alive. They've also helped Lara channel her memories of Adam to help others.

For Adam

In the years that followed Adam's death, Lara never shed the weight of losing him. She struggled with guilt as well, because while he was gone she remained. Adam was the captain of his high school's soccer and wrestling teams, editor of the school newspaper, someone she looked up to.

"I think I had a lot of shame for not being a better person," she said. "I felt like I had to make sure I did something with my life."

In 2011, Lara decided to take her pain and use it to do some good. She devoted herself to kindness for the entire month of October, honoring Adam's memory with thoughtful acts. Adam always had been there for her, someone to lean on. Now she wanted to be there for other people.

Lara paid for strangers' coffee and meals, donated to local causes, gathered a truck full of blankets for a local homeless shelter, and surprised her grocery-store clerk with a candy bar.

"I never know how someone I reach out to will react," she said, "what someone takes away from it, but I put these things out there and hope the meaning reaches the right person. People are very skeptical about receiving kindness. They don't always trust it, but it can really change someone's day when they do."

Eventually she wrote about her effort on her blog. "It was insane," Lara said about the countless people who read her posts about random acts of kindness and offered encouragement. "I couldn't believe the response."

Then, in 2012, at age thirty-one, she told everyone Adam's story.

The brutally honest blog post about why kindness became her mission every October is titled "The Hardest Story I Never Told."

"I am going to tell you a story," Lara wrote. "I haven't done this before, told this story, so detailed and so publicly.

But I am going to try something big this month, and I think I need to tell this story in order to do it well."

The post ended with a promise: "I want to commit myself to honor all the good Adam would have done if his life had not been cut short. I wanted to be just like him when I grew up. Well, here's my chance."

Thousands of people read it, and the post went viral.

And so did Lara's mission.

"The Biggest Kindness of All"

Hundreds of people have reached out to Lara from across the country, and many have pledged to follow in her footsteps. They give back in Adam's name right along with Lara, who started using the phrase "Adams Acts."

Lara eventually added a hashtag in front of it: #AdamsActs.

"This year I'm challenging all of you to do this with me," she wrote on her blog.

It was an open invitation. Adding the hashtag to "Adams Acts" allowed anyone to connect with Lara and others when they were doing something good.

Today a search for #AdamsActs on Facebook brings up a seemingly endless stream of posts about a variety of kind acts. Some are small gestures: buying lunch for a stranger, delivering a homemade pie to a neighbor, placing money under the windshield wiper of a parked car just because. Others are more ambitious: donating an organ to a person in need, organizing a fundraiser for a food bank or hospice, collecting blankets for homeless shelters.

Often a note accompanies the deed.

"#AdamsActs," they read.

Lara has taken her message to elementary schools, where she speaks about the value of responding to life's difficulties with kindness. She's received emails, videos, and letters from people in the US, Europe, Africa, Japan, and India who have joined the effort in honor of Adam.

Adams Acts has brought more light into the world, and it also has helped her make sense of her brother's death. "Kindness, of course, does matter," Lara said. "That is significant, but more importantly, I went through something bad, and I want something positive to come out of it. It's been very powerful. It really gave me permission to still feel grief, to still feel these things. That's very empowering and it's very healing."

Lara said readers of her blog often write her about their own losses. They tell her giving back to others in Adam's name is helping them heal too. It's now a shared experience, she said. "Perhaps that's the biggest kindness of all. We've ended up sharing our hearts with one another, and that's helped so many."

෯

"Spread love everywhere you go.
Let no one ever come to you without
leaving happier." –Mother Teresa

A Year of Kindness

"When you help somebody
else, it helps you really realize
just how blessed you are.."

FOR MONTHS, ANGELA Gaddis, kept the birthday present
she was giving herself a secret.

She'd been quietly working away at it since the start
of the year, putting in a heartfelt effort every day. The
premise was simple: one year of service to others filled
with daily acts of kindness—large and small—in honor of
her fiftieth birthday and also in honor of her father, who
died at that age.

She bought coffee for strangers and picked up the
check for random diners at a restaurant. She volunteered

at a children's hospital and gave money to a long-forgotten acquaintance struggling to make ends meet.

Angela did all this quietly, seeking no attention. Not even her family knew about it. That is, until one day, when she was approached by a colleague at Belhaven University in Jackson, Mississippi, where she's an associate professor of social work. David Sprayberry, the university's assistant director of public relations, asked to talk with her about meaningful projects her students were working on.

He was looking for outreach efforts to highlight at the university. Angela told him service to others wasn't just a department theme—it was a personal journey she had taken.

David listened in amazement as the soft-spoken professor with a Southern accent recounted her efforts. "It was definitely out of the ordinary," he said. "I've never really heard of anyone taking each day and looking for ways to serve other people, but honestly I wasn't surprised. That kind of thing fits her so well."

"We Need to Approach People as Human Beings"

When Angela was three, her parents separated. Her father, a Korean War veteran, suffered from post-traumatic stress syndrome for years and turned to alcohol to cope. By the time his wife left him, he was a chronic addict.

Angela said her mother, a nurse at University of Mississippi Medical Center, made sure she saw her father whenever he was sober. But as a single mother, she struggled, and when childcare wasn't available, Angela often spent the day at work with her.

"I grew up essentially in that hospital, watching my mom and others serve these individuals who were literally on the brink economically," she said.

These experiences left a deep impression on Angela. She learned that judgment should be reserved and help should be given.

She was fourteen when her father died.

"It was not until later that I was able to understand truly the importance of that time in my life," she said. "Now I can say it helped to make me who I am."

Angela knew she wanted to help people. Before becoming a professor, she was a social worker for twenty years, working with physically and emotionally abused children, veterans, and their families.

Being a social worker taught her everyone has needs. "We need to approach people as human beings," Angela said. "When you're helping them, you have to look at the whole person."

As her fiftieth birthday approached, she took stock of how to improve her own life. That's when she realized nothing feels better than helping someone else.

What if, Angela thought, *I did that every day for an entire year? Could I create a lasting habit of service?*

"When you help somebody else, it helps you really realize just how blessed you are," she said. "I wanted to walk away with that knowledge."

On New Year's Day, she woke up intending to reach out to someone that day—and every day for the entire year. She didn't tell her husband or children. She simply made a vow to follow through with her promise to herself every day.

"I just said, 'This year I need to be intentional about how I'm going to serve someone else.'"

Making the Most of Kindness

"Having a dad die at fifty, that makes things very real," Angela said. "I am so blessed to have lived fifty years on this earth. I'm still here."

And she's been making the most of it.

Her days never start with a plan for service to others. Yes, she has organized volunteer efforts, such as helping out at a camp for sick children, but she said she usually just waits for an opportunity to present itself—and they always do.

One day she was driving out of a parking garage when one of her son's former classmates walked over to say hello. He'd grown up playing with her son and eating dinner at her home. He told Angela he was working overtime at a factory, earning money to help his mother.

"We just kept talking and he never complained," she said.

That's when she reached into her wallet, withdrew all the cash in it, and handed it to him. "Do with this whatever you need to do," she told him.

"He just wept," Angela said. "He stood there and wept."

A few months later, she was traveling home from the airport with a friend when she noticed a young woman standing by the side of the road next to a police car.

Angela stopped, got out of the car, and approached the woman, who told her she was homeless. "She said, 'I've got nobody. I've got nowhere to go.'"

Angela connected her with a local shelter where a friend worked, and the woman went to stay there.

"You never know what your help is going to look like to the other person," she admitted.

But part of the fun, she said, has been not knowing

what form her efforts to help others will take from day to day.

"The real fun stuff is the serendipitous stuff that I don't plan," Angela said. "I'm forming a habit of service, and I'm becoming aware of the world around me."

The yearlong effort has brought her joy, and it's inspired David too. It's "the little things" that make a difference, he said, and her efforts are a perfect example of that. "A lot of times we're not looking, and we miss these opportunities to give back," he said. "Angela is looking."

Angela said she hopes her pledge is one others will take on. "I do believe it takes a willingness to put yourself aside," she said. "But then you're able to really recognize and see the needs of others. What would it look like if everybody just took one day and bought someone they don't know a meal?"

❧

"The great acts of love are done by those who are habitually performing small acts of kindness." –Unknown

Layaway Angel Makes Acts of Kindness a Way of Life

"It's for somebody else, but I think I get more out of it than they do. I come to life."

IT WAS A week before Christmas when Cathy O'Grady walked into a Boston-area Toys"R"Us intent on spreading goodwill.

Cathy, her fiery shoulder-length red hair framing her warm smile, introduced herself to the store's manager.

"I want to pay off some layaway purchases," she said in her distinct Boston accent.

It was Cathy's second stop that day. She already had paid off about $2,000 worth of customer layaways at another Toys"R"Us that morning.

But random acts of kindness are a way of life for Cathy, and she hadn't finished for the day. She stood at the store's counter for three hours while staff ran her payments, one by one, through two registers. She paid off all the store's pending layaway purchases: $21,000 worth of items customers had put on hold as they made payments on them.

Although she intended the selfless act to be anonymous, a local television crew got word and showed up to film her. Then a few customers who'd come to check on their layaway items learned Cathy had paid off their balances.

Today Cathy is no stranger to the reaction that even the smallest gesture of kindness can produce in a stranger. She's the founder of Sofia's Angels, a Boston nonprofit dedicated to doing good.

But she still gets choked up and teary eyed when she describes how one woman reacted when she approached the store counter that morning, intent on canceling her layaway purchase of toys she'd been hoping to buy for her two children.

"She couldn't afford to make a payment," Cathy said. "She didn't understand what staff were telling her, that someone had paid the balance. She kept insisting she needed to cancel it, that she couldn't pay for them."

"See this woman right there," a sales associate

finally said, pointing to Cathy. "She just paid for your layaway items."

The woman approached Cathy and fell to her knees. "It was very, very emotional," Cathy said. "It was very humbling."

Cathy believes kindness matters. It's also infectious, and Sofia's Angels is all about spreading it.

Honoring Sofia

In the summer, Cathy walks through parks in the Boston area, placing rubber balls, chalk, Frisbees, and jump ropes on benches for children to play with, and she often anonymously picks up the check for a family's dinner at a restaurant.

If you ask her why she does it, she'll tell you about her mother, Sofia Papadopoulos—the woman who taught her everything she knows about kindness.

Sofia was thirty-nine and a mom of two when the family moved from Greece to Watertown, just outside Boston. Cathy was just seven then; her brother was twelve.

"We didn't have much," she said.

Her parents each held down two jobs. Her father Apostolos washed dishes at night and painted houses during the day. Sofia worked for a shoe company and a local bakery.

"No matter what, even though she was working two jobs, I can honestly say we didn't go to a restaurant until I was in my teens," Cathy said.

Instead, they always had a home-cooked meal.

Sofia also volunteered at a church, preparing meals for families who'd just settled in the community from Greece and donating whatever clothing they could spare to families with even less than her own family had.

Sofia was soft-spoken and generous. "She didn't sleep. She was just constantly in motion, but then, that's when she was happy," Cathy said. "When she was doing for others, she would be happy."

In 1997, ten days before Christmas and after a twenty-year battle with breast cancer, Sofia passed away. Keeping her mother's memory alive became a mission for Cathy.

"I didn't know what to do," she said. "It was always in the back of my mind. I knew at some point it was going to happen. I just didn't know how and when."

Then Cathy decided to take part in a three-day, sixty-mile Susan G. Komen Walk for the Cure, aimed at raising funds for breast cancer research. To raise the $2,300 she needed to take part in the walk, she crocheted beaded bracelets. She sold them online and got requests to make more.

"I have a friend with multiple sclerosis," someone said.

"Can you make a bracelet that serves as a reminder of people with that condition?"

"Yes," she'd say, "but only if I can donate the profits to charity. I don't want to make a profit off somebody's illness. I refuse to do that."

The business, Cathy's Creations, became a nonprofit. Within six months, she was donating jewelry profits to about twenty-five different causes; within a year, she'd given to 130. The jewelry she sold allowed her to make $35,000 to $40,000 in donations.

"Every month, when I would write the checks, it would shock me, but it was a good shock," she said. "It was a happy shock."

One bead, one bracelet led to a movement of giving. And Cathy reaped a reward that can't be measured in currency.

"One of the things that I do feel guilty about is how great I feel when I do this," she said. "There's, like, guilt attached to it because I'm not supposed to get something from this. It's for somebody else, but I think I get more out of it than they do. I come to life."

In Sofia's Memory

Cathy's jewelry business snowballed.

Then the snowball turned into an avalanche.

During a day trip to Boston with her youngest son, Cathy happened upon a homeless man sitting on a bench during a cold rain.

"He had a plastic bag, like a trash bag, for a jacket," she said. "My son looked at me and looked at him and said, 'Mom, why does any human have to have a plastic bag for a jacket? We have so many jackets up in the attic. Can we just bring him a jacket?'"

"I said, 'Buddy, you get it, don't you?'"

Suddenly Cathy realized how she could honor her mother.

She established Sofia's Angels and put the money she made selling jewelry toward helping people.

Her first order of business was to purchase twenty-five heavy moving blankets. She wrapped each of them in a clear plastic bag with a five-dollar gift card to McDonald's and a note.

It read, "We are not lost. If you're cold, please take one and know that you're loved."

Cathy and a group of friends left the blankets on benches, in vestibules—anywhere the needy might find them.

Two days later, the gesture attracted overwhelming attention on social media. News outlets sought out the anonymous, mysterious Good Samaritan after stories about the good deed went viral. By the end of the week, the news about what Cathy had done was widespread.

At first she shied away from the attention, but eventually she relented. There's a fine line, she said, between bragging about an act of kindness and inspiring others to carry out their own.

So she stepped over it.

When a friend's husband died after a 368-day battle with cancer, Cathy carried out 368 acts of kindness in his honor. She bought coffee and subway passes for strangers, left quarters in empty phone booths, put together more than two hundred "nurse survival kits" for the medical professionals who had cared for her friend's husband, and raised money for his family.

"Those small things, they might be small to us, but not to the person who gets it," she said. "It's not a financial thing a lot of times. It's just a spirit lifter, and it always ends up being somebody who needed that."

Spreading "Contagious" Kindness

Tasha Shipe believes one person can make a difference, and Cathy is proof of that, she said. A few years ago, Tasha, a mother of five and a cruise director at BB Riverboats in Kentucky, was waiting tables during a dinner cruise.

"Cathy asked me if anyone was celebrating something," she said. "She wanted to pay for their dinner."

Cathy picked up the check for two other tables—the bills totaled at least $300—left Tasha a $100 tip, and shared the story of Sofia's Angels with her.

"By the end of the night, I ended up in tears sitting with her," Tasha said.

Today Tasha oversees Blanket Northern Kentucky in LOVE, a Facebook group aimed at providing assistance to homeless people in the region. She collects and distributes coats, hats, food, and other items to people she meets on the streets and in shelters.

Cathy is now a dear friend of hers. "It all started with Cathy and saying, 'If she can do this, I can do this,'" Tasha said. "It can be done. You just have to be willing to do it."

Jill Greene agrees. Last year she found out Cathy had paid for her family's dinner at a restaurant. "I had never thought to do something like that for anyone other than family or friends," Jill said. "If somebody can pay for someone else's dinner, can't I do something like that?"

Cathy's kindness opened Jill's eyes to the impact anyone can make, and she decided to follow her lead. She's paid for a stranger's meal, donated to an animal shelter, and handed out items to the homeless. These experience have been life changing, she said.

She also met with Cathy in person to thank her for setting an example. "Cathy's changed my life so much," Jill said. "She's just amazing in that she does things that no one would think to do, and that's contagious."

To date, Cathy has donated more than $100,000 to charitable causes and performed countless random acts of kindness.

"It just makes me feel so good knowing that it affects the other person so much that they continue it," she said. "It's infectious. It grows, and it makes my heart so happy knowing that it started from something so small."

"My bucket is full all the time," she added. "It is."

&

"Fashion your life as a garland of beautiful deeds." –Buddha

Acknowledgments

DETE MESERVE AND RACHEL GRECO

This book would not have been possible without the help and support of so many. First, Rachel and I are grateful for each of the Good Samaritans in this book who've shared their stories with us. We are inspired by all you do and are certain that the world is a better place because you're in it.

We are also thankful for the help of editor Angela Brown whose insights and suggestions helped us hone and polish these stories.

Also, thank you to readers everywhere who share

random acts of kindness stories with us, comment on them on Facebook, and send uplifting emails.

To our friends and family: thank you for encouraging us to write a book that comes from our hearts. Your support—along with your snacks, caffeine, and laughs—truly is the most beautiful act of kindness in our lives.

Author's Note

RACHEL GRECO

This book would not have been possible without the willingness of so many Good Sams throughout the United States and Canada who agreed to share their stories. Although they live in different places and lead different lives, they share a common goal: to make this world a better place.

Thank you to each and every one of you for taking the time to talk with me, for telling me about your efforts, and for sharing your thoughts about kindness and the power of good. Your generosity and strength awe me.

Thank you too, Dete Meserve, who sought me out and shared your vision of creating a book that would lift people up with real-life stories of kindness and goodness.

You're a kindred spirit, and I'm so grateful to have met you and to have received this opportunity.

Lastly, thank you to my family. My husband Tony and daughter Grace encouraged me to pursue this project, despite my unpredictable career as a full-time reporter and the many life challenges that cropped up while I was working on this book. Amid illness and a bit of chaos, they have been my unwavering cheerleaders, always offering support and love. They have my heart, and I wouldn't have been able to do this without them.

Author's Note

DETE MESERVE

I hope these uplifting stories of random acts of kindness have brightened your days.

To read more stories like these, please follow me on Facebook at www.Facebook.com/GoodSamBook, where you'll find thousands of true stories about ordinary people who bring light and hope into the world through their good deeds.

Please also visit www.DeteMeserve.com to find book club discussion questions for *Random Acts of Kindness*. Plus, learn more about my novels, including *Good Sam* and *Perfectly Good Crime*, both of which are mysteries about the search for people doing extraordinary good for others, and *The Space Between*, a novel about a woman rediscovering the love that had been right in front of her all along.

- ***Good Sam*** follows reporter Kate Bradley as she searches for the identity of an anonymous Good Samaritan who's leaving $100,000 in cash on doorsteps throughout the Los Angeles area. **Soon to be a Netflix Original Film starring Tiya Sircar in Spring 2019.**

- In the sequel, ***Perfectly Good Crime***, Kate investigates a series of sophisticated heists at high-end estates, which are connected to large-scale acts of kindness taking place throughout the city. Is someone robbing the rich to give to the needy?

I'd also love to hear about your own random acts of kindness, how you—or someone you know—are making the world better through your acts of good. Please email your stories to DeteMeserve@gmail.com.

Story Updates

Here are a few updates to some of the stories in this book:

"Fraternity Boys Surprise Twelve-Year-Old Cancer Fighter": Lexi Brown passed away on May 4, 2016, after a courageous battle with cancer.

"Good Samaritans Furnish Homes for Former Foster Children": Georgie Smith was honored as one of CNN's Top Ten Heroes in 2016.

"One-Hundred-Year-Old Makes a Dress Every Day": On May 5, 2016, Lillian Weber passed away shortly before her 101st birthday.